T0195023

A Surgeon's Odyssey

JONATHAN MURRAY, M.D.

BALBOA.PRESS

A DIVISION OF HAY HOUSE

Balboa Press books may be ordered through booksellers or by contacting:

Balboa Press
A Division of Hay House
1663 Liberty Drive
Bloomington, IN 47403
www.balboapress.com
1 (877) 407-4847

Because of the dynamic nature of the Internet, any web addresses or links contained in this book may have changed since publication and may no longer be valid. The views expressed in this work are solely those of the author and do not necessarily reflect the views of the publisher, and the publisher hereby disclaims any responsibility for them.

The author of this book does not dispense medical advice or prescribe the use of any technique as a form of treatment for physical, emotional, or medical problems without the advice of a physician, either directly or indirectly. The intent of the author is only to offer information of a general nature to help you in your quest for emotional and spiritual well-being. In the event you use any of the information in this book for yourself, which is your constitutional right, the author and the publisher assume no responsibility for your actions.

Any people depicted in stock imagery provided by Getty Images are models, and such images are being used for illustrative purposes only. Certain stock imagery © Getty Images.

Print information available on the last page.

ISBN: 978-1-9822-3844-5 (sc)
ISBN: 978-1-9822-3845-2 (e)

Balboa Press rev. date: 11/13/2019

CHAPTER 1

The Republic of South Africa

"What the hell do I do now?" I murmured to myself.
"Is there a problem?" Asked the anaesthetist in a quivering voice.

I had studied hard not to show emotions externally but I think it was the way my eyeballs were out on stalks and my forehead broke out in sweats that gave the junior anaesthetist the idea I had bitten off more than I could chew. The normal relaxed atmosphere in the operating theatre was gone. The idle chatter, jokes and the noise of the monitors was absent in my mind, I was concentrating too much.

I was looking into a 35-year-old female's abdomen and saw the liver was in two halves. I had done what I was instructed to do. She came in from a road traffic accident with swelling of her abdomen. Having checked the rest of her and found no other injuries I inserted a needle through her abdomen wall and sucked up fresh blood. Cat scanning and ultrasound were not available at that time. I called my consultant on call, he told me he was busy and just to go ahead and do a paramedian incision to see what was bleeding. I organized the operating room and in a short time she was asleep on the operating table.

"Please give me the handle for the overhead light. It makes it so much easier to have a full illumination of the operating field with this light that does not cast shadows," I asked the scrub nurse.

I duly prepped the patient and then did an incision just to the right of the middle from below the ribs down to her belly button. And then moved the muscle to the side and opened the peritoneum, the tissue covering the intestine.. With retraction there we had it. The liver in two halves. At this stage I had barely done any amount of surgery. After qualifying I did one year in hospitals as apprenticeship and then six weeks of cardiothoracic surgery and now in the white hospital of Durban, Natal, Republic of South Africa. I was placed in a situation quite beyond my training and indeed my expertise. To put it bluntly I hadn't reached the subject in my surgical tome. The anaesthetist suggested calling the consultant, and to my relief he picked up the phone to the consultant explaining the problem.

I did not want to be apparently shaken in front of the nursing staff in the operating room so I talked to myself "don't panic, I hope the consultant comes in from his farm which is 20 miles away in the middle of the night because I am awake at 2am and I need his help."

His reply was "just put a gel foam sponge to stop the bleeding in the liver. Put in a drain and close her up." I hesitantly accepted the advice although it seemed to me at the time too simplistic. I stitched her up and the anaesthetist replaced the blood loss. Despite the air conditioning my gloves were full of sweat and my scrubs were soaking with sweat. I crossed my fingers toes and any other good luck charm I could think of. Sleep did not come easy that night. But lo and behold in early-morning rounds we found the patient sitting up and smiling saying "you saved my life". I did not like to admit my inadequacy but was delighted she survived and in due course left the hospital one week later fully fit. It is a surgical aphorism that it is better to be lucky than good. This baptism of fire was repeated on several occasions.

However the Chief of Surgery, Mr. White, wiped the floor with me for not getting better backup.

"What would you have done if the hepatic artery or the portal vein had been compromised?"

There he was looking very dapper in his white safari suit with short sleeves and long trousers smoking his 10th cigarette of the morning appearing very condescending. Unaffectionally called 'that hooked nose bastard' by his colleagues. Inwardly I thought I would have soiled myself but knowing the culture of the surgical milieu I decided to play the game and replied "I don't know, sir," almost to the point of obsequiousness. He then went into a long involved diatribe to which I nodded my head in agreement although the real answer was to involve the consultant on call who was 'too busy.' I was reminded of the mushroom existence of the newly qualified doctor who was kept in the dark and only allowed into the light to have manure poured over him and put back into the dark. This interface was only the first of many such telling off, most I have to admit were really in my interests to mould a future surgeon.

I recalled a conversation I had with my first surgical consultant during my apprenticeship.

"Mr. Thomson, I am not sure that surgery is my future" I said.

"What has changed your mind, we took you on as a budding surgeon," replied my boss.

"My confidence took a major knock at the final exam in surgery."

"Tell me about it."

"When I was waiting to examine the patient the senior doctor organising the exam told me that the patient thought she knew the diagnosis, but she didn't. I got the wrong diagnosis and then the examiner said I did not examine her breasts properly because I did not take off all her clothes. I had to sit the exam again."

"But you passed so put it behind you, you will be fine."

And so I launched onto a career of interest and fulfilment. I had realised in medical school that although the entrance requirements were stiff intelligence is not needed to be a doctor but a good memory is essential in learning all the technical knowledge; anatomy was my most difficult subject, learning the telephone book was easier.

The adrenaline resulting from this first challenging operation and the fact that the patient survived is probably why I chose surgery as a career. It was so exciting and challenging to more than satisfy my ego. Here I could do what I always wanted to do. If I had stayed in my Edinburgh I would have been studying for more exams and not getting the hands on experience I was rejoicing in. The surgical team at Addington Hospital consisted of a full-time consultant with a few part-timers, a senior resident, a middle grade resident and myself. It seemed that my responsibility during daytime was limited in the white hospital, but suddenly I was super responsible at night. However I was in charge of the wing for the coloured patients. These people were the progeny of several generations of white black mix originating in the Cape colony. I would like to think they were looked after well and I was often complemented on the occasional ward round from the senior consultant.

What was I doing in the Republic of South Africa? I had qualified from medical school and having been born and bred in the same city I felt I had to experience a different way of life.

"I would like to go somewhere else to see some of the world and see different ways of practicing medicine," I asked Mr. Thomson.

"I can fix you up in either Hong Kong or South Africa, which would you like?" He replied.

"I have always had a yearning to see Africa so I would like to go there."

"OK, I will write to Mr. White in Durban, he trained here with me in Edinburgh before going back to South Africa where he came from."

I was heavily criticised by my contemporaries in Edinburgh but as a visiting South African physician put it, I was going to help all South Africans and not necessarily supporting apartheid. Certainly the allure of that subtropical sun all year round to alleviate the dullness of the Scottish weather was very attractive. As the visiting South African physician described his stay in Edinburgh," I wake up and it is dark, I go to work and it is dark, I come home and it is dark, are you all troglodytes?" To be fair to Edinburgers he was only there for the winter.

After qualifying I was let partially free on the unsuspecting public in an apprenticeship. During that time I became more and more interested in surgery. I learned how to take blood and do minor surgical operations like "lumps and bumps" as well as inserting chest drains. The most difficult procedure was to remove a sebaceous cyst from the back of the neck. It is amazing how much blood flows through that area. However surgery was my chosen career and I was determined to follow that course. It turned out to be a hard choice with multiple exams and frustrations and a roller coaster emotional life.

Eager anticipation for the future was probably the best description of my feelings at the time. The White hospital Addington was situated over the road from the beach and the Indian Ocean. Addington hospital was fairly new at the time. It was high-rise and everything gleaned cleanliness. The views over the ocean were spectacular. I am told the glitter has now worn off. We were billeted in a one-room apartment behind the hospital within the Doctors Quarters. The culture of the hospital was relaxed, epitomised by the manner of summoning on call doctors lying on the whites only beach by putting a towel out of a window to alert them. I sought out my overseeing consultant Mr. Alan White. He was about early 50s, 6 feet and upright with a good head of greying hair.

"Welcome" he said." I think you will enjoy being here. I expect a lot of hard work but you should play hard as well. My consultant friend in Edinburgh speaks highly of you. I have made up a rota for you starting with six weeks in anaesthetics, then six weeks in cardiothoracic surgery which is in another hospital and then back here for general surgery."

The bureaucracy of being hired by Natal Provincial Administration seemed never-ending with all papers in triplicate and several signatures required. In fact it took the whole afternoon to complete the process. As a guest worker in a foreign country I did not feel it was my prerogative to point out the non-necessity of this.

The six weeks anaesthetics was incredibly boring because I was merely an onlooker and in those days there was no scavenger equipment to remove all the exhaled anaesthetic gases so I inhaled them and felt sleepy all the time. It is said quite rightly that anaesthesia is 95% boredom and 5% panic.

However that familiar smell of a mixture of anaesthetic gases and antiseptic gave me a thrill. It is quite distinctive and at the beginning of my career was almost orgasmic. I must have been born to be a surgeon.

Cardiothoracic surgery on the other hand was a delight. The hospital was situated on the Bluff on the periphery of Durban at the time. The first day I walked onto the ward to be shouted at by the senior trainee.

"We start the ward round at 7.30, this is your first and last chance to shape up or ship out." For the rest of the morning I tagged along behind him getting a grilling on my knowledge and experience. However I had been schooled in the hard knocks class so was not too perturbed.

"We are doing 3 mitral valve replacements today so you and I will open the chests and the consultant will do the procedure and we will close up," the trainee told me."We will do the left thoracotomy and creep into the chest cavity, controlling the bleeding with diathermy."

"Do you use pig valves to replace the valves damaged by rheumatic fever?" I asked.

"Yes and good, you have done some homework," was the reply.

The consultant surgeon, Professor Ben Leroux who coincidently trained in Edinburgh, was a master, every movement slow and exact, no wasted movement and operations lasted much shorter than I had anticipated. I do not remember coming across a better surgeon whose hands were as gifted as his. Watching him was magical. He was completely bald which was unusual in those days. It was rumoured he shaved his head once a week in the bath. He was complemented by a retired cardiothoracic surgeon who taught him in Edinburgh; Andrew Logan, the father of cardiothoracic surgery in the UK .Perhaps Professor Leroux was rivalled in my eyes by Professor Victor Richards in San Francisco where I was a student for 3 months. He was voted the best abdominal surgeon in the USA in 1972 by his peers. Every movement unhurried and accurate.

It was fascinating to see an open heart pulsing away. Obviously the heart had to be bypassed to allow a relatively blood free operation. This was partly helped by the anaesthetist and a cardiopulmonary bypass technician. This latter was my wife's job. She quit after 2 weeks and I began to realise she and I were not as compatible as I had originally thought; but that is another story.

Back in Edinburgh, the same operation was another matter. The surgeon appeared in the theatre at 9.30 having been at his private practice, donned his rubber gloves and stood waiting for all around to do his bidding. He felt he was given special powers that no one else had and only he could do the operation properly. He regularly berated not just the surgeons in training but also the nursing staff. If he smelled garlic he went mad at any foreign surgeons in training assuming it was them. His rudeness was legion and even the orderlies were fed up. During the prolonged surgery he requested a orange drink which was given by a straw around his face mask. The cup was held by an orderly while he sucked but the orderly pinched the straw making the surgeon red-faced in his efforts. Another dastardly ploy was to upset him. He was a bit short sighted and removed his glasses to shower before operating. One of the orderlies got hold of a plastic dog excrement and placed it on the floor of the shower. In his poor sight he saw the offending object, jumped to the wrong conclusion and came into the operating theatre frothing at the mouth wearing only a towel and accusing everyone. The personnel in the theatre collapsed in laughter. A separate incident involved a surgeon who had prominent ears. The anaesthetist told a very junior nurse to lay out some tape for the surgeon. When it came time to scrub the surgeon asked the nurse the reason for the tape.

"Why, it is to tape back your ears" she replied in all innocence.

The anaesthetist could not control his laughter. He thought "you deserve it, you are such an arrogant bastard, you even wear a bow tie."

I ask you.

As you may know this was the land of apartheid where black and white did not mix.

I asked a colleague about this apartheid business which was totally foreign to me.

"Jim, you are an expat anaesthetist originally from England and you have been here for at least ten years, what is your take?"

"I don't want to talk about it right now but when we finish the operating list let's take a walk along Addington beach."

A couple of hours later we found ourselves scuffing along the beach with the waves gently lapping over our bare feet.

"Why did you not want to talk about apartheid in the operating theatre?" I asked Jim.

"So we won't be overheard. Have you heard of BOSS?"

"No, what is that?"

"It is the Bureau of State Security, like the KGB, omnipresent; walls have ears and any discontent with the present regime is noted and is held against you, meaning either deportation or a spell in Robben Island."

"What is Robben Island?"

"An island off the south coast of Cape Town where Nelson Mandella was imprisoned for trying to stir up a revolution against this white government.

My own feelings are that the South African government made an enormous mistake in legislating the division of races as apartheid tends to occur naturally. In Natal Zulu and Xhosa are the predominant languages of the black races. For instance the signs for elevators and wash rooms are whites or non-whites or blankes or nie-blankes. These divisions border on the farcical when, in one example, identical twins were separated, one designated as being white and the other non-white. One of the most iniquitous pieces of legislation is the pass laws. If a non-white is caught in a white designated area after dark it is assumed he is up to no good and is arrested and put in jail. He appears the next morning in shackles in court and faces his punishment. So no I don't agree with this apartheid but it is not my country and I can't do anything about it. I know some people who have been deported. Some Afrikaaners honestly believe the black Africans are somehow less than human."

I was beginning to learn this at first hand. The cardiothoracic operating theatre was staffed with black and white nurses who worked together on the black patients but when a white patient came in all the black staff had to leave. Soon after I started I attended a meeting at the African Hospital King Edward VIII which finished after dark. I had to get back to Addington Hospital where my apartment was. I decided to take a bus. I stood at the bus stop vaguely noticing there were no white faces around. When the bus arrived I stepped up into the bus to meet a heavy grill behind which the black driver shouted at me "you aren't allowed on this bus!" It dawned on me that I was on the wrong road and that the white buses used the parallel road where I eventually got a ride.

One day the other cardiothoracic surgeon asked me to 'clerk' in his maid who was due to have a minor procedure. I heard the word 'asseblief' so I assumed that that was her name. So I trotted off to the 'black wards' to find Mrs. Asseblief. I was met with totally blank faces. I asked the sisters if they could understand what I was trying to say. After five minutes of dancing around my question they asked who had sent me. I told them and then the light bulb switched on. It transpired 'Asseblief' is Afrikaans for please! Well you got to learn I suppose. Intertribal rivalry was unfortunately part of the culture in this hospital. Depending on the tribe some patients had to pay to get a bedpan while others did not.

Because of the apartheid laws Addington hospital was designated a white hospital. As an addendum a Cape Coloured hospital was attached. These patients were the progeny of the mixing of white and black races originally from the Cape of Good Hope region well before apartheid had been thought of. The most common diagnosis was acute pancreatitis. The main cause of this condition was alcohol. When asked how much was drunk the inevitable answer was it was 'only a bottle of spirits a day. However the size of the bottle was 2 L and the alcohol was almost pure.

My next module was surgery in general. This included abdominal surgery, plastic surgery, pediatric surgery neurosurgery and vascular surgery. Actual hands-on training was very dependent on which consultant I was working for and there were several different personalities. One day a 21-year-old male came in to casualty with a 12 hour history of upper abdominal pain. A routine abdominal x-ray showed he had air under the diaphragm which is diagnostic of a perforated duodenal ulcer. As I was very junior at the time I called my consultant who was at his ranch several miles away. I got the distinct impression he was not in any hurry to come to the hospital.

"What are you going to do?" he asked over the phone.

"What do I do?" I asked plaintively. "I had hoped you would come in to do the operation."

"No need, I am busy here. You can do it. Just do a paramedian incision(a vertical incision slightly to the right of the midline of the abdomen) through the peritoneum find the perforation and suture it and suture some omentum over the ulcer" was the reply." I am 40 minutes away so by the time I get there you will be finished. Call me if there is a problem. But don't do anything stupid," he added ominously. The omentum is a skirt of fat within the abdomen.

I had never organised an emergency theatre before. I had never done anything like this before so I approached the head of the theatre.

"You need to book the emergency theatre, but I hear a fairly major car accident is coming in so get a move on.. You also need to get the anaesthetist on call."

The anaesthetist on call was also a trainee but he felt confident to go ahead.

"We need to cross match him for blood just in case things go wrong," he said.

Another delay with the news that the road traffic accident victims were beginning to arrive in the emergency department, speed was the essence to avoid being bumped to operate at a later time. My anxiety reached previously never visited levels. For some confidence boosting I went to the hospital library to revise the anatomy I was going to encounter. Eventually the hour of action arrived and the patient was wheeled into the operating suite. I checked his name tag to ensure we had the correct patient and a breezy smile of confidence from the anaesthetist greeted the subject of the exercise.

"Just a little prick" commented the anaesthetist as he slid a small needle into the back of the patient's hand. He injected some anaesthetic agents and the patient was asleep in seconds.

"Thank goodness for that" breathed the anaesthetist, "this is the first one I have done by myself and to say the least I am nervous."

"That is nothing compared how I feel," I replied.

I painted the abdomen with betadine containing iodine to sterilise the field and with the assisting nurse put on the drapes to isolate the operative field.

"Here goes," I said to myself.

I incised the skin just to the right of the midline from just below the ribs to below the umbilicus. The next layer was the covering of the six pack muscle the rectus abdominus which I cut and moved the muscle to the side and clamped the next layer and elevated it to avoid cutting the underlying intestines, incised and entered the abdominal cavity. NOTHING happened. I recalled as a student being joked that a huge amount of gas would come out. So I moved the intestine around and sure enough there was a small hole the size of a 1 cent piece in the duodenum. I sutured the perforation and the omentum in place, washed the cavity with saline, inserted drains in case of contamination and closed up.

"A real baptism of fire" I thought to myself.

The operation actually went perfectly well. I'm glad to say the patient recovered quickly and his convalescence was uneventful. The surgical aphorism of 'see one, do one and teach one' was never more apt. Unfortunately on this service the first step was often omitted.

For instance I was asked to see a 10-year-old boy in emergency department. He had all the clinical signs of appendicitis. I had never done an appendectomy before, in fact had never even seen one before. There was no senior surgeon available so I just went ahead by myself. I had a quick read up in a surgical atlas and went ahead with the operation. Again I was lucky in that I found the appendix almost immediately delivered it out of the wound tied off the blood vessels put a circular suture in the caecum and removed the appendix. After that a nurse told me the whole procedure 'skin to skin' took seven minutes. It is better to be lucky than good! Most of the time I was assisting, retracting tissues and cutting sutures. Thus I acquired knowledge and experience. One tedious assisting was in gall bladder removal i.e. cholecystectomy. The Deaver retractor was metal with a wide end to retract the liver and it was held by a narrower part of the same metal. Depending on the surgeon the operation took an hour or so. Apart from painful hands and with all the action out of sight at times I almost fell asleep on a few occasions. Nowadays the operation is done through keyhole surgery with fiber-optic instruments cutting the operating and recovery time considerably.

I guess urology was my bete noir. I have said some of the worst surgeons were egotistical. My time in urology was a nightmare. I couldn't do anything right, even to the point of pouring coffee wrongly.

"You are useless, you will never be a surgeon, give up now before you do any more harm," he shouted on more than one occasion. That was like a red rag to a bull. From then on things got worse and I curtailed my time there before there was bloodshed.

For recovery we toured northern South Africa, visiting Kruger National Park, crossing into Rhodesia at Beitbridge, onto Salisbury, then Kariba Dam, took a ferry to Victoria Falls, on to Bulawayo and eventually back to Durban. We thought at the time Rhodesia was one of the best countries in the world. Now look at it.

Orthopedics was what I wanted to do long-term and managed to get transferred to that service. This was much better and the adage was 'see one, do one, teach one.' At least I saw one before doing one. Unfortunately putting in a pin and plate for hip fracture, or putting a prosthesis for a femoral head was not challenging enough for me to last all my surgical career. The other thing that put me off was when we did surgical rounds the consultants started shouting at each other swapping insults and generally misbehaving. Not for me, thank you.

The surgical personality is strange and I speak as one. I mean how can you take a scalpel to a fellow human being having just been joking with him in the anaesthetic room minutes before. The refuge is to think 'this is a piece of meat that has to be made better.' In some surgeons I think it is a mixture of an over inflated ego and insecurity.

Then I was drafted to the intensive care unit (ICU)for the hospital. It included medical and surgical patients. Thank goodness obstetric and neonatal patients were treated in their own intensive care unit. I would not have had a clue if I had to look after them. As it was my medical knowledge in that specialty was pretty basic. Things went not too badly until we had a death and he was a candidate for kidney organ donation. Although he had a pathognomonic sign of death with 'tracking' of his retinal vessels meaning the blood vessels in the back of the eye showed interruption, he still had movement of his limbs. Thus ensued a heated argument whether he was dead or not. Finally it was decided by those greater than me to insert iced water in both ears. A negative response, as opposed to the eyes flickering which is called nystagmus, confirms death. The organ transplant program was just starting so preparation did not go smoothly although at the end the operation was a success. The society in Natal at that time was fairly violent and assaults and murders were not uncommon. After a middle-age man was stabbed and died in the ICU the police wanted to interview his wife. She said she was too busy to speak to them the next day as she had to go to work. I would like to think she was shell shocked as I could not get my head round the callousness that the woman did not care.

One evening I was studying in my apartment when the phone rang. "You'd better come and see this" said the nurse in charge of the emergency department.

"My goodness" or words to that effect I said to myself. There was this man with the broken off kitchen scissor blades sticking out of the top of his head. The x-ray showed the blades went half way into his brain. Incredible force must have been used to plummet the weapon into his cranium. This was definitely beyond my expertise! I called in a neurosurgeon who shaved the head removed some surrounding bone then very delicately extricated the offending foreign body. There was a very real risk of torrential bleeding but lo and behold it did not happen and when the patient recovered his only pathology was an inability to see peripherally. What a let off!

Doctors are human and like everyone else make mistakes, it is inevitable. However what is not inevitable or acceptable is laziness and ego. While I was in ICU we had an unexpected admission from the operating theatre. A 60 year old male was having a cancer removed from his bowel when there was a sudden profuse bleed. The surgeon did not tell the anaesthetist because they did not speak to each other. It was too late for the anaesthetist to make up for the loss and the patient subsequently died. Another female 12 year old was in ICU after a road accident with multiple injuries. She was on a ventilator but when she was swapped to another ventilator the nurse forgot to check the machine. The result was she did not get enough oxygen and she died. A 35 year old male was admitted to the hospital with a stab wound severing his femoral artery. He was given too much fluid at surgery and died. This case went to court and I had to give evidence. In the end the accused was found not guilty because the defence lawyer argued that they were playing with the knife which just happened to fall into the victim's groin. I made a note to use that lawyer if I ever needed one!

There was my fair share of horrendous sights like having to certify death in an African whose body was cut in half when he was run over by a train, or a climber who fell in the Drakensberg mountains and broke almost every bone in his body.

. I found the doctors in the White hospital aggressive compared with those in the African Hospital. Some of the junior staff trained for the Comrades marathon. This was an annual race but not of 26 miles but 56 miles, the start alternating between Durban and Pietermaritzburg. From Durban the race was uphill and downhill from Maritzburg. The training was in the very early hours before the sun was up. Not for me.

My next stop was to work in the gigantic African hospital. There were beds for 2000 patients but there were about 4000 inpatients. The solution? Mattresses between and under the beds on the floor. In fact you could do a ward round without touching the floor, only stepping on mattresses. Some so-called patients slept in the hospital, breakfasted went to their day job and returned at night to eat and sleep. My first day in the operating theatre started at 8am and finished the next morning at 8am having assisted at 8 operations for abdominal stab wounds. There were many more chest stabbings with consequent pneumthoraces (holes in the covering of the lungs giving collapsed lungs). The treatment for these was to insert a drain into the chest and let the air in the chest cavity out under a water filled jar. On a daily basis a long line of patients with these drains wandered through the surgical wards doing their physiotherapy to encourage reinflation of the lungs. The main problems seemed to be intertribal assisted by the ingestion of large quantities of homemade maize beer (juba). The main combatants were Zulus from the north and Xhosas from the south. After one holiday weekend by chance I visited the city morgue. There were about 50 bodies piled on top of each other, the result of 3 days celebrations. Life was cheap. Interestingly I got more tuition at the African hospital than at the White hospital.

My seniors were very nice people and great teachers. Being the bottom of the pile in the surgical team I was assigned to draining abscesses of which there were many. At the time I had grown a flimsy moustache and after a week of this duty I noticed a constant smell wherever I went. It eventually dawned on me the cause of the smell which was alleviated with the disappearance of the hirsutism. One difference from western medicine was the treatment by witch doctors (songomas) who danced and threw bones to the floor to heal their patients. There was no double blind placebo controlled trial to justify this approach. This whole African experience stood me in good stead for my future career. The difference in staff attitude between the white and African hospitals was palpable. In the white hospital there was a lot of rivalry and animosity with back biting. The approach in the African hospital was one of 'we are all in this together so get on with it.' I think a lot depended on the personalities of the chiefs of staff. While I was there we had the Soweto riots in 1976. The violence in the Johannesberg townships was contagious but thankfully did not spill further south to Natal. One of the most heinous crimes was a depithing. In the overcrowded trains to and from these townships passengers were forced to stand and hold on to overhead straps. While they hung malevolent enemies took a bicycle spoke and rammed it between the lumbar vertebrae to depith the spinal cord resulting in lower limb paralysis. This crime attracted the death penalty. The intertribal violence amounted to a civil war and on one occasion I came across an Emergency doctor who was so phased out by the threat of violence he felt he required to carry a gun. Of course the Zulus are a war like nation by tradition so transformation to peaceful living within a few generations could not be expected. One of the idiosyncrasies of medicine in the field was the 'jova'. Some self styled unqualified 'doctors' gave out injections to poorly educated Africans to help them service as many wives as possible. I think these were just vitamins but seemed to satisfy their recipients.

"Jim tell me more about apartheid," I asked on another occasion walking along the beach.

"The problem of apartheid is one that mystifies the rest of the world. I can understand it to some extent. Here were the persecuted from France Belgium and Holland fleeing to the Cape of Good Hope to set up a colony free from interference. No sooner had they done this than the British came, ousted them and the Great Trek took them north to establish another colony in the Transvaal. The Afrikaaners then set to suppress any other threats, which were the African nations. Their mistake was to legislate. It was easier to keep the repression but as history will tell in the future once the lid is removed all the underlying resentment explodes to civil war as seen subsequently in South Africa, Russia and other countries. On the other hand when Britain gave up control of Rhodesia, Mugabe installed horrendous authority over the black tribal population with intimidation and violence against the white population, in particular seizing land from white farmers. As well he perpetrated genocide of rival tribal groups notably the Matebele tribe. The argument I have heard from those who have no idea what they are talking about say Africa should be for the Africans. In fact the original inhabitants of Southern Africa, the Hottentots have largely died out or remain in South West Africa. Around Durban, Natal the demographics have placed the white population in the middle surrounded by Indians who were imported from South India and Ceylon, the Tamils, to harvest sugar cane at the turn of the 19th century who in turn were surrounded by Africans. The result was the Cato Manor riots of the 1950's when Africans fought the Indians but the whites were protected..

There are four races designated by the Government at that time namely, Whites, Cape Coloureds, Indians and Africans or Blacks. So there you have my feelings about South African politics, but it was a great place to live if you are white."

One of my most enlightening experiences was meeting a General

Practitioner who took over a large area of Zululand. Prior to his arrival the diet followed by the locals was appalling with well overuse of sugary carbonated drinks, lack of vegetables and with a prevalence of tuberculosis in 50% of the population. He showed the natives how to grow vegetables themselves rather than buying them, decreasing the unhealthy soft drinks, and teaching them how to fish wisely. As the Chinese proverb says 'give a man a fish and you feed him for a day. Teach a man to fish and you feed him for a lifetime.' With this advice and encouragement he reduced the level of tuberculosis to 2% of the population without medication and the general health was increased considerably. There obviously was a lot of resistance to this wholesome approach by both the medical profession and the natives but it is a shame that it was not adopted more widely.

At the time one of the medical mysteries was the apparent wasting of the body mainly restricted to African males. For no known reason the condition rendered previously healthy men undergoing a loss of weight to eventually lead to death. There was also a coincident outbreak of Kaposi's sarcoma a type of skin tumor. We now know these conditions were caused by the virus which today is called the AIDS virus. At the time this was untreatable, but thankfully today it can be controlled.

At the end of my stint in South Africa on my last day at the 'black' hospital I went to say goodbye and thank the surgical team for the experience. I parked in the hospital car park. It was about noon when I had finished and I jumped in my car put it into reverse and I suddenly heard a scream.

"Crickey, I have just run over a dog" I thought. I leapt out of the car went round to the back to find an African trying to get out from under the rear end. He had been sleeping under the car to be in the shade of the noon day sun. I got such a fright I lifted the whole back of the car up by myself to let him out. He had the tire mark of my rear wheel over his forehead. Thankfully there was nothing wrong with him but thank goodness for the Zulu toughness.

To become a surgeon at that time there were two professional exams to pass. The first was called the primary fellowship and the second was the Fellowship to achieve the magical letters after your name of Fellow of the College of Surgeons. There are three colleges in Great Britain, Edinburgh, Glasgow and London. I was studying in South Africa to sit the primary which is common to all colleges. I was told on several occasions that no one had ever passed the primary from Durban, you had to come from Witswaterand(Johannesburg) or Cape Town. I studied in my spare time. Our apartment was one bedroom with a verandah at sea level and in the summer was very humid, so studying was very unpleasant. . With this difficulty I was unsure about our future. However I paid the fee and sat the written in Durban. I was totally not confident about the result. The oral part was in Cape Town and being chronically short of cash I was in a quandary about flying there. After a lot of self examining I made up my mind to go"' I may as well try for it although I have been told the pass rate is only 8%." The day before I left the telephone kept ringing in my apartment. I was on a day off so I did not want to be called in so I did not answer it. On the plane the next day, I met another doctor going to the same exam. His exam was on that day so his brother-in-law was to meet him in a fast car at the airport to take him to the exam. I got a lift with them knowing my exam was the next day. To my horror when I arrived at Groote Schuur (Big Barn, the hospital where Christian Barnard performed the world first heart transplant) I found my oral exam had been moved to that same day which was the reason for all the telephone calls. Maybe it was just as well that I did not have time to become too nervous. The anatomy and pathology were okay. In physiology I was asked fairly straightforward questions such as what colours urine and what causes high blood pressure. Here I learned inadvertently how to handle oral questions. I rattled off the common causes of high blood pressure and somewhat hesitantly mentioned phaechromocytoma which is an extremely rare cause of high blood pressure. It is a tumour of the adrenal glands secreting adrenaline. Many years later I examined for the Surgical Fellowship of the Edinburgh College and found it extremely boring. If a candidate said something esoteric I would latch onto that to really test them. As they say 'if you're in a hole stop digging.' This is what happened to me. I did not tell the examiners I had just written a scientific paper on phaechromocytoma so I started talking and talking and talking until the bell went to signify the end of the exam. "I see you qualified from Edinburgh, I qualified from Glasgow," said an examiner.

My normal riposte would be,"You have done well despite that" but I did not think it would be appropriate given the circumstances so merely nodded in agreement. I did not hold out much hope but was delighted to get a phone call two days later to say I had passed.

To finish my time in South Africa I did a locum on a sugar farm up the coast in a small town called Stanger. So peaceful and relaxing compared with the hell on wheels of a busy hospital. While I was working my wife and the baby played on the local beach and at 2 PM everyday a school of dolphins swam past and put on a show for them. Idyllic.

One of my clinics was quite a bit inland. I was to ensure that the prevalent conditions of high blood pressure and diabetes were in control in the Indian population. My uniform was a pure white safari jacket and shorts with knee length white socks and white shoes. The clinic was controlled by a 6 feet 5 inches coal black refugee from Mozambique whose mother tongue was Portuguese and had only limited English. If the patients did not respond to his directions his solution was to shout louder. The patients all had a test tube full of their urine to be tested for sugar. Unfortunately a patient while having the pressure cuff attached managed to pour all of her urine on top of me. At this I decided to reorganise the clinic to avoid any further situations.

The Africans were employed to cut down the sugar canes and such was the heat and vigorous activity the average fluid loss of the workers was about 20 litres a day. They replaced this loss with large quantities of weak maize beer (juba).

There was tragedy even in a backwater when a 9 year old diabetic boy went into what was subsequently found to be a diabetic ketoacidosis coma. His grandparents thought he was in a deep sleep. He died. I was the doctor summoned to investigate the problem and was quite distressed to find he had passed. Despite the hardening I experienced in the African hospital this got to me. I saw several conditions which were rare in Western medicine including a florid case of syphilis and a baby dying from measles. One night I was driving back from the sugar farm to the hotel we were staying at by some back roads. It was as dark as the Earl of Hell's waistcoat with driving horizontal monsoon rain. In my head lights I spotted an old African lady valiantly struggling against the elements on the way home. As any reasonable person would, I stopped and offered her a lift. She sat in the front passenger seat and we went on our way. After only about 200 yards we came across a road block. With a flashlight (torch) in my eyes an Afrikaans accent "what are you doing here and why is the African sitting in the front seat?"

"I am just driving back to my hotel and gave her a lift to her home in this bad weather," I replied. The bulky policeman turned to his colleagues and entered a lengthy discussion. After quite a while I was dismissed. I subsequently discovered I should not have let the African lady sit in the front; another lesson learned that my culture did not always work in this foreign land.

Social life was so much better and relaxing than in Edinburgh. We were introduced to Braaivleiss (Afrikaans for barbecue), Castle and Lion lagers and a feeling that we deserved to relax and certainly not the uptight Presbyterian culture of Scotland. The denizens of Durban knew how to relax and enjoy life. The ocean was a great playground. I tried surfing but was so inept that I was soundly told off by the lifesavers never to do this again. I think you have to start this sport as a youngster to be any good. Perhaps it was just as well as one day while swimming at Umhlanga Rocks I was taken offshore by the undertow and had to wait before being thrust back to shore by powerful waves. Shark nets close offshore were supposed to protect surfer but occasionally they fell short with consequent loss of life and limbs. Nevertheless enjoyment was as much of the culture as was hard work.

The rest of the world was quite rightly extremely intolerant of apartheid. However the media reporting was not always fair. Two weeks after coming back to Britain I saw a television programme filmed on the very sugar farm I had been working on as a doctor. The Africans claimed there was no medical support which was a total lie and wrongly reported. The reporter said he had to support the antiapartheid movement hence his biased comments.

CHAPTER 2

ENT training

B efore leaving Edinburgh I was told "You will never get a job back in Edinburgh if you leave now," by one of my consultants an overweight red faced arrogant Englishman.

I have to say that my response to this consultant's negativity would be to say there are many other places in the world to live. I landed a job in three days time in ear nose and throat surgery otherwise known as otolaryngology head and neck surgery which is what I really wanted to do. I was immediately hired as I was the first Edinburgh graduate for 12 years to show an interest in the specialty. I chose this because the surgery was challenging, involved children, I would not have to wait for patients to take clothes off to be examined and there was relatively little night work.

I went to the City Hospital where the inpatients were housed to be told to appear at the Royal Infirmary the next day at the outpatient department.

I asked to see the two consultants and shook hands with them. One who would become my long-term mentor was about 5'9" tall balding and running to fat in his early 40s. Dr. GD I will call him. I subsequently learned he did a spell in America and after a short while he moved to Edinburgh.

Fairly dynamic, he had all the characteristics of a small man. Aggressive, pushy and not concerned about hurting feelings. He asked me why I wanted to do ear nose and throat surgery and I explained all the different fascinating facets of the job which he agreed with. In South Africa I had been exposed to several different surgical specialities and felt ear nose and throat would suit me. The only problem that I could see was that I already had a job doing six months in radiotherapy which had been organized by my previous consultants.

"Don't worry about that, I will fix it, but can you start tomorrow?" He said.

I should have picked up on that at the time to realize what sort of person he was. My previous consultants who had fixed up the radiotherapy job were incensed, quite rightly but with some smooth talking I survived. However I started and it was really like learning a new language. The only two subjects I had failed in my medical school were surgery and ear nose and throat so it was a challenge to overcome those obstacles psychologically and get a grip of the subject. I did receive several reprimands from the powers that be from the health board for not doing the radiotherapy job but to be fair Dr GD dealt with them telling them that I was the first medical student from Edinburgh to do ear nose and throat in the last 12 years. So now I was looking to develop expertise in the subject that seems to encompass all types of surgery including routine tonsillectomy's middle ear problems, hearing problems in general, cancer work as well as cosmetic work.

The training was again a bit haphazard, for instance the training in tonsillectomy was the same 'see one etc.' but the technique is quite different from general surgery. Using instruments deep in the mouth took some getting used to, but with time it became routine. I have heard many times that removing tonsils is easy, but usually from people who have no idea what they are talking about. There is still a mortality rate from the operation so it is not to be sneered at. Similarly inserting a ventilation tube in the ear drum necessitates a unique technique which does not come naturally. Interestingly both these operations have been put under scrutiny in the UK and there is talk of not allowing them in the National Health Service.

Head and Neck surgery is a lot more akin to general surgery as you can handle tissue and you are not operating down a hole although these operations are more glamorous than the smaller operations. The major ear surgery was mainly performed by the consultant under a microscope and the junior staff watched down a sidearm. How we were supposed to learn the techniques was beyond me. However we could practice on cadaver temporal bones in a laboratory. It was a lot easier to drill into the mastoid bone and look in the middle ear in an inert subject. The first bone I drilled into showed me how little I knew of the anatomy and was a hopeless mess, but I am told that this experience was shared by many of the top ear surgeons in the world. Again time and patience were the keys and eventually it came right.

When operating on ears and the nose there is little room for 2 surgeons so a lot of the instruction is verbal and from books. It is up to the individual surgeon to learn much by himself, certainly that was my experience. It reminded me of my chemistry teacher at High School whose aim was to teach us boys to teach ourselves.

There appeared to be the old school approach of some of the senior surgeons who scrubbed their hands preoperatively until they were raw in the thought this would kill all the germs. In fact more recent knowledge shows that this only uncovers more germs so today the scrub is not so severe. Another change is in the atmosphere in the operating room or theatre as it is called in British based hospitals. The senior surgeons were bullies and regularly shouted at junior medical staff and nurses. Today this would result with a walk-out.

The outpatient's at my lowly level involved sitting in a tiny enclosed area called horse boxes, which were just flimsy wooden cubicles about four in a row, with the patients. Conversation was easily overheard by waiting patients. It was less than ideal but in fact I learned a lot from my immediate colleagues and in particular an almost retired ENT registrar. After a few years I sat and passed the Fellowship exam for the Royal College of Surgeons of Edinburgh. One incident sticks out in my mind during this exam. In the ENT practical I was examining the patient with a bedside table on which I had a small lit spirit lamp to warm the laryngeal mirror I was using. I was concentrating so hard I omitted I left a paper on the table. After a few seconds I realised I had set the paper alight and I got such a fright I pushed the paper to the floor and burnt the floor covering. I did not burn down the hospital but the mark remains to this day. The irony is that it was quite possible to pass this exam which was designated as the beginning of training without ever using a scalpel. For some reason I attracted several opera singers during the Edinburgh Festival most of whom wanted an injection of calcium to improve their singing voice. If I gave them calcium it would probably have killed them so instead I encouraged them to drink copious amounts of water before singing in the dusty atmosphere of on stage. As soon as I moved on my mentor moved in to take over the care of these opera singers and made an international name for himself. Over the next few years I got on fairly well with my mentor particularly when he discovered we had gone to the same school and achieved the same athletics championship. In my personality I learned to keep my mouth shut even when things were not particularly fair. I had also started writing scientific papers while in South Africa so I was well accustomed to doing so in this job. It had been pointed out to me many years before that one has to make one self unique to stand out from the crowd to progress. Dr GD suggested I look into nasal fractures as nobody had done much work on this before. I was allowed to set up a nasal fracture clinic on a Monday afternoon to collect the weekend's trauma. Having suffered from several nasal traumas playing rugby myself this was a subject dear to my heart. Over two and a half years I collected over 1000 cases, probably the largest number worldwide at the time. I started doing my MD thesis. In those days this was a fairly uncommon degree to have and it was deemed to be the highest qualification available from Edinburgh University. And over the years I learned more about Dr GD much of which was unpalatable.

CHAPTER 3

My mentor

With menacing clouds of Mussolini's fascism gathering over Italy in the mid-30s, the bourgeois intelligentsia of the country were becoming increasingly restive. The thought of enforced enlistment outraged one particular young man. Giuseppe had a beautiful wife and a newly arrived baby who gargled away to himself; GD was named after his paternal grandfather as he was the first grandson. Every day newspapers and radio thundered out the message that things are changing and the family knew they were not changing for the better. On September 1936 having prepared for several months, they left their apartment in Perugia after the evening light had gone, carrying two suitcases between them. That was all they could take of their possessions. They left behind many of the special memories which meant so much particularly in the difficult times that lay ahead.

Apparently confident but inwardly extremely nervous Giuseppe led them to the railway station. He knew there was a train bound for the Florence leaving at 11 o'clock. At the station he bought return tickets to Florence mumbling to the ticket seller something vague about visiting an aunt. He could feel the sweat on his brow and under his arms. After 20 minutes the train pulled in and he got his family and suitcases on. What a relief when the whistle blew and the train pulled out of the station. The first stage of the journey! Baby GD gurgled away to himself, totally unaware at such a tender age he was about to undergo the second most dangerous journey of his life; the first was his descent through the birth canal of his mother only a few months before.

After Florence was Milan, and across the border to Berne, Switzerland. There after the situation was not so tense. The family were terrified that they would be stopped and returned to face long-term imprisonment or worse. After two days of travelling they ended up in Edinburgh, Scotland where, they had heard there was a slowly increasing community of displaced Italians. They were welcomed into the 'family' and quickly found jobs. Giuseppe was an accountant and his wife sold ice cream. Like many immigrants they were driven to make a better life than the native Scottish. The years went by and with the skill of Giuseppe and engaging personality of his wife they slowly accrued enough money to put a down payment on ice cream shop in the high street in Musselburgh which is near Edinburgh. With increasing affluence they felt they wanted the very best education they could afford for the baby because they were determined to make him an achiever. He seemed quite bright so the age of 4 ½ years they took him to sit the test for admission to one of the fee paying private schools for which the capital is well known. GD was a bit intimidated when he entered the gates of the school with tennis courts in front, then the parapets, then the building itself. It was said that the architect modelled his drawings on the Kremlin and it certainly gave out sinister vibes. He passed the test without a problem and attended the school for 13 years during which he excelled both academically and in sports.

GD had been imbued for all his formative years that medicine was the only profession to enter, and with single-mindedness passed all the relevant hurdles to enter Edinburgh University medical school. He was even more determined to succeed. However medical school was quite a strain and he had to study hard, almost as hard as the female medical students. In those days there were few females in medical school but they studied twice as long as the males because they felt society did not fully accept female doctors.

Eventually in 1959 he qualified MB Ch B to great celebrations within the Italian community in Edinburgh. On qualification he felt his original name was not fashionable, particularly after the war no matter that his family fled the fascists. He decided to change it by deed poll to another closely related name which was not such a huge change. However during the time of his medical school he remembered the ending of World War II and his burning ambition to be someone special was fired. He could see the opportunities for leveraging himself up the social ladder in his adopted country which seemed ripe for the picking.

"Surgery that's what I'll do," he decided and hence started on the long hard road to be a surgeon. The first year had to be spent living in hospital, working most of the time. He had managed to get only peripheral jobs, eschewed by the University teaching centres, but this did not bother him as he had the "the Grand Plan" in his mind and he knew when to make his play. Nevertheless the hours were long, but laundry and food were provided by the hospital, although the salary was pitiful. The only way he could survive was from handouts from his increasingly rich parents. He was getting more and more interested in the politics of Scotland. He sensed a second rate cousin effect from England, which added to a sense of injustice at his such poor working conditions. This only underlined his ambition to take control. In his sparse off-duty he attended as many Scottish National party meetings as possible making quite a name for himself. However he settled down to continue his career until he made the grade of consultant. This is where I came in. I had a broadly similar education as GD but I was several years younger.

The difference was he did not need and I did need summer jobs to fund my way through university. These included delivering newspapers, and milk, labouring, scaffolding, grouse beating, washing dishes on a cruise boat on the River Rhine, picking hops and working in a brewery. I think this was good training to be exposed to all sorts of society before entering the closeted middle class of medicine.

CHAPTER 4

Further ENT training

I n any surgical training there happens amusing incidents. One of mine was to encounter a patient from a psychiatric hospital who managed to swallow a FOB watch which stuck in her upper esophagus. It was easily seen on X-ray and indeed it removed fairly easily but after 4 days in situ it was still ticking! Thankfully ENT is a relatively acceptable topic to talk about in society.

One of the things that irked me was my age. I was passed over for promotion because "I was too young." I qualified aged 22 and had more experience than older colleagues who were promoted above me.

At one stage in the training I was seconded to a peripheral hospital. This was an old Prisoner of War camp in the Second World War. It consisted of several huts and while operating you could see a field of cows immediately outside. The infection rate was surprisingly extremely low. The consultant in charge there had just resigned so I was left to get on with things for the most part. Again teaching myself helped a lot. I appreciate this goes against surgical dictum but it seemed to work out and anything not specifically within my experience was referred to the main hospital. But I really enjoyed the freedom. The theatre was dedicated to ENT which was great. I was also well assisted by a nurse Joe Brown a Tynesider with a wealth of ENT experience guiding me through some difficult operations. He said he knew if I managed to place the stapes prosthesis properly because I inadvertently held my breath at the 'moment critique' of the middle ear operation. The retiring consultant had a beautiful phrase 'a consultant makes the same mistakes as trainees but with more confidence'. A patient had a typical story of a subdural abscess but it was not recognised. Unfortunately he stopped breathing and I intubated him and transferred him to the neurosurgical department of the Royal infirmary where unfortunately he succumbed. Many ENT operations are very short. Indeed one day when most of the other surgeons were tied up elsewhere I was allotted 2 theatres for the morning and another session in another hospital for the afternoon. I walked between theatres as the anaesthetist put the patients to sleep and operated to leave the patient recovering as I went to the other theatre to operate. At 3pm I had performed 35 small operations. These included the now infamous guillotine tonsillectomy. For small children the patient was put to sleep, the mouth was kept open with a gag, the left tonsil was surrounded by a snare and the operator used a finger to bluntly dissect the tonsil. The same for the right tonsil and a scraper removed the adenoids behind the soft palate. The patient was turned on his side with cold water sluiced over the face and the torrential bleeding miraculously stopped. All in all it took 19 seconds and the rebleeding rate was very low. I am glad that operation has been abandoned.

Until then I never realized how surgeons are taught. As a medical student you are regarded as a bit of embarrassment, tolerated but not to be taken too seriously, not infrequently chided. But nothing compared to the systematic degradation inevitable in the training of a surgeon. My previous experience had been very gentlemanly with the exception of a surgeon trained under the Scottish system. I suppose the idea is to make one 'battle hardened' to withstand the inevitable criticism of making life-and-death decisions. GD was a classic. He was a good teacher but a very average surgeon. Going into the operating theatre with him made your pulse leap, your blood pressure soar, and before soon you sweated buckets under the sheer nervous tension. There is a classic question a surgeon in training asks "do you want the sutures cut too long or too short today?" He epitomized that approach. Your hands started shaking uncontrollably, such that even tying a knot with a suture was an uphill struggle. The difference between him and other surgeons was night and day. On one occasion he left me to do a radical neck dissection when he was attending some meeting or other. I was in the middle of the surgery when I got a message that my wife had gone into labour. I could not leave the operation but felt a bit unnerved. However I finished the operation successfully but Dr GD next day exploded at me for cutting into the face. The incision was definitely not in the face. He recanted the accusation later but no apology ensued. His Mediterranean temperament produced unpredictable behaviour which was very unsettling for his trainees. In retrospect I think he was unhappy with his domestic life. Also at the time his naked ambition for the Scottish National Party leadership had reached and passed its zenith as his colleagues found him too much of a zealot. He did not seem to realize that in his adopted society one did not want to appear too ambitious, one had to be coaxed into a position of power rather than seize it. He tried for other positions of power including University and the civil service but the same rejection applied as Scotland is a village in these circles. He played golf and the piano in an effort to impress and joined the best clubs.

CHAPTER 5

New Zealand

I had always wanted to travel so for the next step which was a consultant post I was appointed in New Zealand in North Island, Palmerston North. The joke about the airline pilot on approaching landing at Auckland airport was "ladies and gentlemen as we near landing there will be a time change, please turn your watches back 20 years" was not inaccurate. Having travelled half way round the world we, that is my wife and four children under the age of five, arrived pretty jet-lagged. After a night's sleep I ventured to meet my new colleagues. Having waited for twice as long as normal for the older of my 2 colleagues to finish a tonsillectomy he came out of the operating theatre with his gloved hands contaminated with blood and offered to shake my hands. He then proffered" I think you should go home to Britain because there is nothing here for you".

"But I have just travelled half way round the world," I said.

"Best you leave," he replied.

To say the least I was taken aback. He followed this up in due course with a strong attempt to have me fired. He went out of his way to be awkward and to unsettle me. I think he felt very threatened. Fortunately for him I treated a bleeding tonsillectomy patient after he had operated and left nowhere to be found. There were several other incidences when he had to be helped out of difficult situations of his own making. In general he was past competency and I wrote a letter to the Hospital board pointing out that he should not be allowed to operate. This was received with a large degree of paranoia. So I was summoned and asked to rescind the letter. I was offered head of department if I did so. I refused. A patient was left with a large but operable laryngeal tumour to die in his home 2 hours from the hospital. The patient came into the emergency department in extremis going blue. As no-one could find the relevant surgeon who happened to be on call I was called and relieved his symptoms with an emergency total laryngectomy. I became a Fellow of the Australasian College of Surgeons having sat the exam in Auckland.

The medical staff with the exception of my ENT colleagues were very sociable and regularly held parties. One colleague lived on a nearby farm and his family lived the 'good life.' They kept some livestock and in the middle of their party for medical staff their horse wandered into the kitchen, a common occurrence we were assured. I was offered some pork chops which were donated by their pig. Apparently my colleague and his wife managed to get their squealing pig into the bath where they silt its throat, then doused it with scalding hot water to remove the hair. The chops were tasty until I heard the bath story. The social topics at the time were rugby, racing and beer. There was a huge gender gap at these gatherings. One day the oncologist said he was going to Gisborne on the other side of the island, and would I like to come. I agreed because I wanted to meet the local ENT surgeon who trained in Scotland. I did not realise he was going to fly in his own plane. So early on the appointed day we went to the local airport and pushed his two seater out to the runway. As we taxied he said "We go through that gap in the hills but the weather does not look good so it may be a bit rough. " Well he was not exaggerating, we were bounced up and down for hours it seemed, although the rough patch was only about half an hour.. He handed me a newspaper. I did not know whether to read it, do the crossword, or throw up in it. When I arrived in Gisborne we went to lunch but all I could stomach was two Valiums and a glass of water. When we eventually got home I was told I was looking green. My children went to school in bare feet, quite different. We also coincided in Wellington with the arrival of the QE2 liner which was commanded at the time by a neighbour in Edinburgh, Alex Hutchison. When we were on the bridge a fog horn sounded which was strange in the balmy sunshine. This was repeated on several occasions and eventually we discovered my son was at the exact height to press the button. Mystery solved.

My job involved driving to Masterton in the Wairapa every week which took 2 hours each way. I did operations in the morning and out-patients in the afternoon. In retrospect this was dangerous if a patient had a post-operative bleed. However this seemed to be quite acceptable. One of my patients regaled me with a story of feeding his pigs with marijuana, the growing of which was very illegal. "But it gives a great taste to the meat", he explained.

Another incident did not endear me to New Zealand. When our furniture arrived on the dock it was decided to unload the container there with the result a lot of damage. When I complained I was brushed off by being told to claim it off the insurance. Unfortunately the damaged goods were not covered.

At the time my mentor from Edinburgh wrote saying that a colleague in Edinburgh had unexpectedly retired and would I like to apply for his consultant job. My initial thoughts were no as we were just beginning to settle and the day before the letter arrived we bought a house. I was also offered a job in Wellington the capital of New Zealand. After some considerable discussion I was persuaded to go for the interview. So I returned to Edinburgh a week before the interview against my better judgement. Having been shown around new facilities I was still unsure and on the day of the interview met my mentor and told him I did not want the job. He went apoplectic. I decided to take a sleeping pill get some rest and fly to London to get a flight back to NZ. After2 hours I could not sleep so I thought to myself I may as well go to the interview. So I arrived in a drugged state and my mentor told the committee what I had said to him earlier that day. In a could not care less manner apparently I gave a fantastic interview and got the job. However it did not begin for 3 months and rather go back to NZ I sent for my family. In the meantime I needed to fund this trip and organized to go to the Kingdom of Saudi Arabia until the job started.

CHAPTER 6

Kingdom of Saudi Arabia

Saudi Arabia occupies most of the Arabian Peninsula with the Red Sea and the Gulf of Aqaba to the west and the Persian Gulf to the east. It contains the largest land desert in the world i.e. the Rub Al-Khali or the Empty Quarter. The oil fields are mainly on the east coast near Dharan. The capital is Riyadh with a population of 5.45 million where I gave several lectures. Jeddah is situated on the Red Sea and is the second biggest city with a population of 3.58 million where I did a locum. Mecca has 1.6 million.. I also worked in Tabuk and Aramco near Dharan. Jeddah was the most European of the cities, but even so the women had to cover up. The abaya was a loose cloak and the face minmally covered by a hijab or a larger chador, or an even larger niqab or a full face covering with a burka. The males wore a white body thobe with either a small white hat, a taiga, or a guttra, a large square cloth held in place by an igal, a doubled black cord which originally was used to hobble camels in the desert to stop them wandering off. The religion is Islam and other forms of religious worship are frowned upon. Only Muslims are allowed in the sacred cities of Medina and Mecca. Every Muslim wants to visit Mecca at least once in a lifetime. The entrance port is Jeddah and along the Corniche tents are erected to house the pilgrims on their Haj journey to touch the Kaba in Mecca. Mosques abound throughout the country and devout worshippers pray 5 times per day. The law is Sharia which by western standards is very strict. It includes women having to cover their heads and not allowed to drive. This latter is being relaxed just recently. They continue to have capital punishment and removal of a hand is the punishment for theft. The right hand is usually chopped off meaning the left hand is used to clean the bottom after a bowel motion as well as being used for eating. Stoning to death is not uncommon in cases of adultery. Alcohol is forbidden to Islamists. Many of these laws originate in the nomadic lifestyle of Arabians in the desert before cities were formed and make sense as alcohol dehydrates resulting in death in temperatures upwards of 50C. These temperatures made walking on asphalt extremely painful the searing heat coming through the soles of the shoes. Speaking of which it is considered very rude to show the soles of the shoes while sitting down, why I don't know.

Saudi Arabia was the source of wealth at least according to several colleagues who had abandoned the UK for apparent greater incomes and no tax but not revealing the atrocious conditions a different life style and religion bring with them. Several prestigious physicians left the UK in search of a few years of work to achieve early retirement. I had been there several times before for short periods, and indeed I managed to finish my MD thesis on one visit, probably because there were no distractions of medical politics and family. These short locums did not expose me greatly to the idiosyncrasies of Muslim life. I was sent to an army hospital in Tabuk in the northwest region of the country in the middle of a desert. The Red Sea was a few hours by road to the west and Jordan to the north. My first orientation day was a tour of the hospital. I was told that IBM was installed. Wow, I thought, that is very progressive for this time of early development in computers. No I got it wrong. It is Inshallah, Bokra and Mellish. Roughly translated means "By the will of Allah, Tomorrow, Perhaps" The surgery was pretty standard and little different from Western medicine. There was a problem with language as I had no knowledge of Arabic and had to depend on a non-medical translator. A simple question seemed to initiate a prolonged conversation between patient and translator and usually ended with the response of yes or no. I had to assume the translator was being honest and giving me the correct response. Sometimes this was not adequate but overall things seemed to go reasonably well. On the other hand the patient did not always seem grateful. There was a corporal who managed to sustain a fracture of his face and needed the displacement reduced and fixed. I had no experience of maxillofacial fractures as that was a different specialty where I trained. In conjunction with a dentist we wired the fractures back in place. On awakening from the anaesthetic he started to complain about pain. Despite adequate analgesia for normal patients he continued to shout "Alum Kateer". So he was christened as such which in English means severe pain. In fact he was so unhappy he fired me to my relief and asked one of my colleagues to take over. That lasted about a day when Alum Kateer fired him and wanted a third surgeon who lasted a few hours. No more surgeons were available so I was hired again. Eventually he improved. My immediate colleagues were an Egyptian, and a Californian, Then there was the American who hit his windshield in a car accident. I was asked to see him in the Emergency department. He had a few superficial wounds on his face which I sutured and discharged him. Within minutes a hospital administrator appeared.

"You cannot discharge him."

"Why not, there is no medical reason to keep him in hospital" I replied.

"The Saudi government reckons that if he had not been there, there would not have been an accident so if you discharge him he will be put in jail. We will keep him in Hospital until we sort out the problem." Such a waste of money and quite contrary to Western thoughts about bed usage.

One day I was operating for a deep seated infection of the mastoid bone. There is a large vein behind the bone which in this case was abnormally placed forward. I transgressed the vein and blood exuded. My operating nurse saw the blood and promptly fainted. There was no problem in dealing with the bleeding but the nurse was a different story. Such is life in the OR.

Then there was the social aspect of life. The Muslim religion bans alcohol. However at a Western party homemade "Siddique", literally "My friend", was served being extremely strong alcohol. For whisky, oak chips were added and for gin, juniper berries were used. I have never seen so many hangovers with the shakes in the morning after as there. Indeed on the supermarket shelves grape juice was placed beside yeast and a book called 'the blue flame 'which gave instructions how to ferment the liquid. One day I visited a local palace. I had never before seen such unadulterated gross wealth. In the bedrooms all the fixtures were solid gold of a very high carat value, the bath, shower, taps, even the wastepaper basket was pure gold. A solid gold console dropped down from the ceiling for television and DVD entertainment. A visit to the local gold souk was another eye opener. I had not seen so much gold on show, every store filled to overflowing with high grade gold. It was somewhat disconcerting to see the 14 year old guards standing on sentry duty brandishing submachine guns.

Snorkelling in the Red Sea was a delight. The fish were plentiful and highly coloured darting in and out of coral and the water was ideally warm. My visits often coincided with Ramadan, the month of denying eating or drinking during daylight hours. It ended with the festival of Eid which was similar to our Christmas. The sight and smell of markets filled with herbs and spices were memorable. However when prayer time was called all the stores were forcibly closed and monitored by the religious police. Woe betide any transgressors. Also a western celebration of Christmas was banned or held in a muted fashion behind closed doors. I visited Rastanura on the Persian Gulf where the beautiful golden sands were juxtaposed to the ugly machinery of oil production. This was the site of future conflict during the Gulf Wars resulting in several wreckages blocking sea routes. I travelled over the Empty Quarterr to Al- Hofuf with one other passenger in a Boeing 747 plane. The sight of the undulations of the desert and the pipelines was dramatic.

Life was incredibly boring so there was a considerable amount of promiscuity between all ranks. Indeed every Friday being the Muslim equivalent of Sunday a bus ran from the hospital to a nearby aerospace compound. When the bus stopped about a dozen middle aged men were arranged in a semicircle. When the nurses got off each was paired with a man for the night. Some of the nurses were in their twenties and stunning but they craved fun. Such a waste. The bus was locally called the "fuck truck." I was married at the time and studiously maintained my marriage vows. However if I had been a bachelor....Well! I was extremely relieved when my stint was over and flew home. At Heathrow I called my wife. She informed me that the house we bought before going to Saudi Arabia was full of dry rot despite being surveyed which was to have a hugely disruptive effect on our lives for several years to come.

CHAPTER 7

Edinburgh, ENT consultant

It was a bitter home coming. It would not be true to say that Saudi Arabia did me any good, even the financial rewards did not compensate. The news that repair of the dry rot would wipe us out financially led to near suicidal thoughts. Coupled with the fact that I was entering a very competitive field work wise was extremely unsettling. While I was in training in Edinburgh there was no thought of trying to keep me down but Oh! How that changed when I became a threat to my new colleagues. The salary I was offered was reasonable by most standards but I wanted to educate my children to the highest standard I could which meant going to private fee paying schools. We chose a private school similar to the one I had been educated at. In the midst of the repair work the plumber decided to stop his work and left us with a stand pipe in the kitchen but no other water. This was extremely inconvenient for washing ourselves, clothes and dishes but most of all flushing the toilet. My oldest son was overheard telling his friend that to flush you had to fill a bucket with water, take a deep breath in and, hold it, rush in and pour the water into the toilet and rush out before taking another breath. This state of affairs lasted 2 to 3 weeks. The actual repairs took 2 months and I was grateful that we negotiated a lesser bill which was manageable.

Life continued in a routine manner and I became more settled. Part of the deal I had made with the local health board was I was paid at the 2 year level of the consultants' salary. When it came to the bit they refused and I was paid at the beginner's salary which left a bad taste in my mouth. Also the consultant who persuaded me to return from New Zealand had agreed to take me as a partner in his private practice with an agreed salary. I entered this without any qualms but as time went on it was obvious he wanted me as a lowly paid servant. This only lasted a few months when we agreed it was not working out so we decided to split. Meantime a new private hospital was being built so I had 3 months of trying to build up my own practice with little extra income to pay school fees. Quite a nail biting time. Also this consultant deducted tax from what he paid me but I had paid the tax and he refused to refund the amount to me. He kept threatening me that I would not get a 'merit award' if I did not do his bidding. These financial merit awards were instituted to control the power of consultants and were handed out by the inner circle. I was told I had to raise one million pounds in research grant money to get an award. I did this but no award was forthcoming. In fact I heard subsequently Dr GD stopped me getting an award. This was very unfair so I increased my private practice to compensate to fund my children's education. All in all not a great start to my career as a consultant. My job entailed working at the City hospital for inpatients and Bangour hospital for in and out patients, out patients at the Royal Infirmary of Edinburgh and organising out patients in the Borders. Subsequently Bangour was replaced by the new St John's hospital. This was supposed to service the new town of Livingston, with some inhabitants of Edinburgh and Glasgow. It was expected by the planners that there would be a huge expansion of the population but this did not happen so that a lot of the services were moved from the City hospital to fill St. John's 35 miles away. From the ENT point of view we lost our autonomy in the theatre and had to share with other specialities. The operating nurse manager accused me on several occasions of being slow in operating but nothing could be further from the truth. The time taken on an ENT list is usually the anaesthetic but the nurse obviously had no experience of my speciality. I decided to increase my private practice not only for the money but for the freedom of working for myself without the constraints of jealous colleagues. Part of this was a company I set up called Hearing Scotland. This entailed doing hearing tests on people whose hearing had been damaged by exposure to excessive noise. In practice this meant testing mainly coal miners. To improve efficiency I made a template for the reports on my computer which was far advanced at the time.

I decided I had to make a name for myself so super specialized in the facial nerve. This nerve supplies movement of the face. I then went to Bordeaux to the 4 yearly world conference on the facial nerve. I picked up a tummy bug there and had to rest in bed for a day on my return. Unfortunately while I was ill disposed the house went on fire. Despite many protestations on my part not to store wood paper and matches beside each other for the wood burning stove they were not separated with the result a conflagration was the result. In the garden in my pyjamas I waited for the fire brigade who did a good job in quelling the fire. The fire chief then blasted into me for bad housekeeping which was a bit unfair as I had tried to avoid the problem. That night because the house was uninhabitable the family went to stay with friends. The windows were smashed out so I stayed with the dog to prevent burglary particularly as the neighbourhood contained several criminals.

Recovering from that was difficult but by now I was somewhat immune to disasters and I got on with life. Work was difficult in that my fellow consultant dreamed of being a moving force in the world of ENT and regularly went off to conferences. To be fair he was a good speaker but his ambition well outweighed his talent. He was very politically motivated and I felt he had an inferiority complex. He was brought to this country from Italy to avoid the Second World

War and his family were never really accepted in Edinburgh society. He was determined to be accepted but never lost his Italian roots, with all the bad traits of his countrymen. There was a continual struggle to assert myself against his overwhelming influence. He expected me to cover him when he was away but did not reciprocate. I was working so hard I was exhausted at the weekend and was not fit for socializing. So I felt pressure at work and at home, not a pleasant existence. I seemed to get a headache on my way home from a busy day but never realised why until later. Although I knew something was wrong I could not prove anything. Relations with the father-in-law were not good. He was a small odious control freak with a huge chip on his shoulder. He interfered with our marital relationship and we had several disagreements. He tried to bully my son to stop him from coming on holiday with me. He also accused me of being a bad parent; considering the mess he made of parenthood I thought this was ridiculous. He subsequently developed Alzheimer's disease and passed. I think he had had the condition for a very long time. Eventually after 5 years of this when I knew something was going on. My wife was a cardiopulmonary bypass technician and was exposed to many surgeons. I thought she would realise the commitment to be a surgeon was huge. She knew this when we married but alas things did not work out. I think her thoughts on marriage were quite different from mine. My understanding of my marriage fidelity vows were they were sacrosanct but obviously I got that wrong. My life had been made miserable with problems both at home and at work so I decided that this was no life. I left the home for good. The revelation that my marriage did not work out was devastating when I thought all that I had done for the family to be treated like this was intolerable but in some ways at least I could relieve myself of the uncertainty and proceed to the next stage in life. It was if a heavy load had been taken off my shoulders. My deepest concerns were the children. Unfortunately as I discovered from my lawyer she would have all the rights of custody .The law really is an ass. I think euphemistically that we were not suited. My children suffered the most.

As the years went on I expect you think Dr GD would mellow; not a bit of it. He became worse, and with it came cloudiness of judgment. More and more mistakes were made with patients with bleeding postoperatively or wrong structures cut. His ego began to outweigh his clinical judgement. He had a row with the operating theatre manager with the result a patient's operation was needlessly delayed. I had to have a word with him to grow up and settle their differences. The patient got their operation. By this time I'd also achieved consultant status and as I worked closely with him I was to some extent responsible for his actions which concerned me greatly. He still had not achieved the recognition he felt he deserved. His ambition was like a nagging duodenal ulcer, constant, flaring up on from time to time but always there. He became very increasingly frustrated that he was not making headway on the various ladders to stardom he had envisaged would lead to an accepted level in society. Then he had his epiphany. "Of course, the Surgeons College".

His clinical work by this time had deteriorated so much that I encouraged him to join as many committees as possible to get him out of the way of patients. In fact I instituted proceedings to make him a Professor. He seemed to forget that in subsequent years. Those were the days when it was quite 'infra dig' to rat on one's colleagues. One had to be a lot more subtle. These are changed days indeed today. Another decade passed and he trudged his way through the ranks by a mixture of plodding and obsequiousness. Then on his 59th birthday he was elected to be president at the college of surgeons.

"I have made it!" He thought to himself. From my point of view this was a great relief. He was now removed from clinical work and was no longer a threat to patients. For his term of three years he felt he had worked hard enough to get a position of importance so he sat back.

I had been upset by him so many times that I had come to the end of the road with him. I had supported him on his very frequent absentees claiming to give very important lectures, looked after his patients and pulled him out of operative disasters. He was a showman and gave very convincing lectures but did not stand up to questions well.

One day I was operating at a peripheral hospital when I got a telephone call.

"Come quickly this patient is bleeding to death."

I sped along the motorway at the fastest I could and in the operating theatre I found a doctor sucking blood coming from a tracheostome site. That is a surgical hole in the trachea to bypass the voice box. Dr GD had operated on a 19 year old female's vocal cords for some reason which I never found out. This doctor's attempt to control the bleeding was as useless as a chocolate fireguard and as soon as I appeared he made some excuse and left. I knew what the problem was. Dr GD had placed the tracheostome tube too low and it had eroded the innominate vein. I put a finger in beside the tracheostome tube to compress the innominate vein and called for a thoracic surgeon stat, meaning immediately. Thankfully one arrived and opened up the chest and tied off the vein. I think my training in Cardiothoracic surgery stood me in good stead in figuring out the problem because Dr GD did not have a clue about the problem.

CHAPTER 8

Social Edinburgh

I had made friends with a local general practitioner doing a fitness class. He above all kept me straight going through the hell of divorce. We trained together and ran a marathon. Well the week before, I tore a medial meniscus in my left knee and could not straighten my leg. I had never been so fit before or since, so I hobbled or walked around the 26miles and 365 yards. The meniscus was removed the following week. My mantra at the time was to repeat 'never again' on the training runs. He also persuaded me to go trekking in the Himalayas which was very interesting but not to be repeated. Soon after I began to develop a lot of gas and abdominal swelling. This provoked embarrassing situations. In private practice the norm was to wear a pinstripe suit with collar and tie. In between patients I had to alleviate the build up of gas. This entailed leaving a window open in the consulting room no matter the weather. The gas was expelled through this window. I had a hard job explaining why the window was widely open when it was snowing outside.

During this time I took up fly fishing with another friend. This was so relaxing to have to concentrate and push my worries to the back of my mind. I had the same experience playing my favourite sport, squash.

I was asked to be the ENT doctor to the Scottish Rugby Union. This was fun as I got behind the scenes and met several international rugby players. When the Rugby World Cup was played in Britain I was given two tickets to watch Scotland playing England at Murrayfield. I took my 10year old son who was dead keen on the game. Unfortunately England won but after the game we were invited for the after match reception. I introduced my son to a lot of the players and he collected signatures and programmes. When I returned him to his boarding school he could not wait to rush off to tell his friends.

CHAPTER 9

Continuing consultancy

Meantime, work was forging ahead and apart from the usual head and neck cancer and routine ear and nose work I initiated some fairly extensive operations including removal of the petrous temporal ear bone for cancer which involved blocking off large veins around the brain, then a week later removing the bone separating from the brain and doing a radical neck dissection removing all the neck nodes and internal jugular vein and subsequently joining the facial nerve, parts of which had to be sacrificed, to the hypoglossal nerve so that the face moved when the tongue was pushed sideways. To my knowledge this was the first in Scotland and the other major surgery was to open the skull via a shield of skull bone in front, push back the brain and remove the ethmoid sinuses from above to remove cancer. Following a conference in Rio de Janeiro, where I got the idea, I introduced the use of botulinum toxin (Botox) to the UK in the management of facial palsy. The idea was to weaken the good side to even up the face with less distortion. I was appointed as part time senior lecturer which is the equivalent of associate professor. The next step up would be full professor but I looked at a few and decided I did not like the job hence did not pursue it.

Professional jealousy arose when I began to clash with a

colleague. The very nature of a surgeon means he has to have an ego because the ultimate critic is nature. In many cases this can be to the detriment of patient care. He and Dr GD were constantly at war with each other which did not make for a smooth running service. Probably personalities were a major factor. In the meantime I wrote several scientific papers, 75 in peer reviewed published journals. I also wrote another thesis on the rat facial nerve to gain a Master of Surgery degree which was the equivalent of my MD or a very good PhD. This was recognized when I won the Masters medal for the best UK research program in ENT. Dr GD was given the medal to give to me. I am still waiting after 25 years to at least have a sight of it. When I asked for it he claimed it was sent to the engravers. This was awarded for my work in the facial palsy clinic. I am a believer that to combine expertise produces the best results. In my facial palsy clinic, the only one in the UK at the time, I brought in a plastic surgeon, a cosmetic ophthalmologist a physiotherapist, a speech therapist and a social worker all lending their respective expertise to give the best treatment available.

After I was awarded the research qualification I thought of all time I had spent on researching scientific papers so founded ENT NEWS. This was a monthly publication with abstraction articles written by the senior registrar trainees throughout the UK. It was distributed free to all ENT consultants to easily keep them up to date with progress in the speciality. It continues to be published to this day and is translated into Spanish. Other specialities have followed suit. I also invited a plastic surgeon to combine in a head and neck operation. The outcome was excellent but my mentor went off his head as he thought that head and neck cancer should be dealt with by only ENT surgeons. To demonstrate my specialty does a lot of head and neck cancer work the title has been renamed otolaryngology head and neck surgery. I was also asked to give a lecture to the British ENT society in the Royal Society of Medicine in London.

One day I was operating when I got a telephone call. "I am a reporter for The Sunday Express. Why are you going to see Gaddahfi, the Libyan leader when he is responsible for so many killings?"

"I don't know what you are talking about" was my reply.

It turned out that one of my colleagues agreed to see the despot but said it was me who was going. The newspaper had front page news about me but as usual got my name wrong.

My junior staff were on the whole very good and enthusiastic. I eschewed the ethos of bullying and took them fishing and skeet shooting on occasions. I was rewarded with being high jacked on my 40th birthday for a celebratory party.

At the time I could see how the NHS was progressing or rather regressing and started a MBA course in medicine. Either I got it wrong or the course administrators got it wrong but I was appalled at some of the ideas they came out with. I don't think they got it right which is borne out today with the NHS in all sorts of a mess. As time progressed the British government introduced managers to the NHS. I could not agree with this move. These managers came from the likes of Tesco and Walmart with no idea how to deal with medical and nursing problems. For instance I asked to meet the manager, Paul Taylor, at one of the hospitals I worked at which he totally ignored. He accused me of taking an illicit holiday when in reality his staff overlooked my completed and accepted application. I had absolutely no respect for this manager. On the other hand mini medical politics raised its ugly head..Some of my colleagues wanted a new extra consultant although there was no justification for one. Despite the acrimony the candidate was appointed. My colleagues waited until I was away when they had a meeting during which they spent the whole day deciding how to get rid of me. The exposé in a Sunday newspaper claiming I was not paying my ex-wife alimony was coincident soon after. This was obviously rubbish and I sued the paper and won. My lawyer who had represented over 2000 cases including surgeons found I was paying more than twice any other cases he was involved in. The divorce took 10 years and $100,000 in lawyers' fees. With all this pressure etc. and the government running the NHS I decided the time to leave had arrived. In retrospect I was equivocal about returning to Edinburgh from New Zealand so from that point of view I was not too unhappy. The phrase' if you are not upsetting someone you are not doing your job was apt on several counts. I think that the medical profession needs regulating as any other profession, but over regulating tries to stamp out original thoughts. The classic example is with the discoverers of Helicobacter pylori. Prior to the finding by doctors in Perth Western Australia it was thought no bacteria could survive in gastric hydrochloric acid. They were almost struck off for challenging the long held dictum. Now it is found H.pylori is present in at least half the world population and may cause erosion of the stomach lining resulting in ulcers. As medical students we were regaled with detailed descriptions of several operations for gastric and duodenal ulcers most of which carried major complications. Triple oral therapy has replaced all these operations giving a saving of hospital costs and improvement of patients' recovery.

The penultimate bitter pill was the Inland Revenue reckoned I owed them 20,000 pounds. I thought this was wrong as I had employed an accountant to do my books. They hounded me until I employed a third accountant to clear it up. The Inland Revenue eventually admitted they had made a mistake and apologised. The last stimulus to leave was the loonies in the Scottish National Party. I refuse to live in an independent country with higher taxes than the rest of the UK. Having been brought up by a Welsh mother and a Scottish father, both of whom were born in England, I have never felt Scottish but do feel British.

CHAPTER 10

Bermuda

In the meantime I had done some locums in Bermuda and was encouraged to return by a anaesthetist who I had taught when he was a medical student in Edinburgh. I was offered a permanent job with a work permit for 5 years. The islands are situated 800 miles east off the Carolinas not in the Caribbean. Life was somewhat difficult there to begin with the threat of independence from the UK raising its ugly head and I thought it was likely this was a temporary job situation. From the academia point of view this move was suicide but I had had enough of Scottish politics, medical politics and the quite unreasonable demands from my ex-wife. But there were problems with this job. The incumbent ENT surgeon had been involved with a post-operative death from a tonsillectomy so I had to overcome the bad reputation and it took some time to establish confidence in my competency. Near the beginning of my stay a Portuguese girl bled a little after a tonsillectomy. Many Portuguese from the Azores are employed in Bermuda. I learned my first Portuguese word 'calma' to her mother meaning don't get worried it will be alright which it was. Another young patient started crying before her operation sobbing "I don't want to die". One of the odd situations arose when patients wanted to be sent abroad to see properly qualified specialists inferring I was not properly qualified. In fact I was better qualified than most North American specialists. As a side issue, I went to see the tax people before beginning to work and asked them to explain how income tax worked.

"You tell us what your notional salary is and we tax at a rate of 8%." Was the answer.

The notional salary had no bearing on the actual salary. The situation has now changed with a much higher tax rate. I was at the peak of my surgical career and the incumbent ENT surgeon wanted to retire despite the fact he was younger than me. After some bitter recriminations I agreed to pay $300,000 for the practice if he would stop working as an ENT surgeon. So this lasted a few years then some black doctors brought in a poorly qualified black ENT surgeon who elsewhere in the world would not have been allowed to practice as a specialist. Anywhere else it is required to have a higher surgical training certificate which he did not. Then the ugly head of racial discrimination began to take over the island which did not help the island as a whole. The chief of staff who was black seemed to be racist in that he did not like white ex-pats. He never had a good word for me and kept suggesting I refer my patients to this poorly qualified black ENT. He subsequently developed Alzheimer's disease which I suspect he had suffered from for a long time before he passed. I gained the Fellow of the American College of Surgeons degree as well as three other American Fellowships. Operating in the King Edward VII hospital was quite different from my previous experience. The anaesthetists seemed to run the show and decided who would gas for who, which was very contrary to me. I, as a surgeon, was in control of the patient as I brought him into the hospital and looked after the post-operative follow up. This approach of the anaesthetists produced considerable friction not only between the doctors but some operating room nurses felt they owned the doctors and the patients. At one stage one of the nurses asked me how she could control me. A red rag to a bull! I refused to have her anywhere near my operating room. This led to a strike action which paralysed the hospital for an hour. The nurses' trade union were brought in and I was forced to apologise but deep down I felt this nurse had a mental problem which needed treatment. Thankfully she resigned soon after. Another episode resulted when a different nurse told me very proudly that nothing went wrong under her control. Soon after, I needed a drill to open up a mastoid bone. When I asked for one this nurse had to admit the drill had gone missing, probably thrown out inadvertently with the laundry. The standard of anaesthesia was very variable with several setbacks which was a totally new experience for me and I had to wonder what sort of place I had come to. I was frustrated when asked to train some OR nurses how to assist in simple operations. I felt this was the responsibility of the nursing profession.

Most of my patients were great and it was interesting to find very uncommon tumours. A patient had a benign ossifying fibroma in her maxillary sinus which I had seen only once before. I came across a benign tumour of the internal jugular vein presenting as pulsatile tinnitus. The irony of that situation was that the patient immediately on hearing my explanation decided to seek a second opinion in the UK. Thankfully he was sent on to an expert in this surgery and the tumour was removed successfully. The general public view of the medical profession in Bermuda was poor, overseas referrals were very common. I was told by many patients that the hospital had always been a source of concern. There were several other uncommon tumours. The causative theories ran from genetic from inbreeding to the effects of coral surrounding the islands. Another patient swallowed a chicken bone. Normally this would have passed down to the stomach with no symptoms as I had experienced several times previously. In this patient the bone stuck halfway down the oesophagus and penetrated to produce an abscess. Thankfully a general surgeon had experience of this and drained the abscess into the oesophagus without needing major surgery. In twenty years experience I had never seen or heard of this before. There was a steady stream of facial injuries from road traffic accidents. The rules of the road were difficult for Americans to understand. Driving on the wrong side of the road was just the beginning. Going round roundabouts otherwise called circulars totally confused tourists as they stopped on the roundabout to allow incoming traffic enter which is quite the opposite of UK based rules. Unfortunately there is always someone to betray trust. An American lawyer from Los Angeles incurred a bill for over a thousand dollars and gave us a cheque. When he left the island he cancelled the cheque. I thought about complaining to the California licensing body but felt they would not be interested in any investigation. At one stage I was the chairman of the Bermuda Medical Society and as such had multiple dealings with the insurance companies who represented the vast majority of the populace, there being no structured state organisation. I was high profile because of this, appearing on local television, newspapers and radio. It arose that because the insurance companies were very slow in settling up claims the doctors had to resort to billing the patients directly. The result was the insurance companies somehow managed to get a law passed to prevent this and all hospital billings could only be put through the insurance companies. It would appear the law of estoppel applies meaning the government could not be sued. Very unfair!

The social life in Bermuda was fantastic. I loved sailing which I did with a great crew almost every Sunday. My first experience on a yacht was traumatic and almost put me off for good. I was told to do the foredeck with a heavily accented Bermudian. I had no idea what to do and with the wind howling could not understand his instructions. Then I was appointed to the winches requiring much less knowledge. One of the crew kept shouting 'tail.' Well the only tail I could see was the skipper's wife which I thought somewhat inappropriate. I subsequently learned it meant to pull on the rope from the winch. When I arrived in Bermuda I bought a 35 foot yacht, never having sailed before.. The learning curve was steep and I learned by making mistakes. The description of a boat being a hole in the ocean into which money was poured turned out to be very apt. My high point was to share in delivering a boat from Bermuda to Newport, Rhode Island. The Bermudians know how to enjoy themselves with regular parties and barbecues. We also had a small motorboat which we used to anchor in Paradise lakes, a well protected lagoon from wind. Many prisoners from the Boer Wars who died from typhoid were buried there. My children came out to visit me on several occasions. One time I went swimming with my oldest. Halfway across a bay I informed him there were sharks nearby. You never saw the speed he reached dry land. Bermudians understand money. My bad experience was when I wanted to sell a motor boat and asked a boat dealer if he would sell it. Nothing happened for many months despite my calling him for progress. One day a patient came into see me and told me her friend was enjoying my boat. So I called the boat dealer.

"Have you sold my boat yet?"

"No, the market is very slow>"

"How come such and such has bought the boat and is enjoying it?"

"Let me take this call in another room. Well things are slow so I was going to pay you as soon as I had the money."

"But you have the money so I expect the money in cash on Monday, otherwise there will be repercussions. Just because I am an expat does not mean you can cheat me."

The money arrived on Monday.

I also enjoyed the freedom to practice medicine without the interference of meddling colleagues. Of course there was one administrator who thought I was too successful and tried to stop me. In fact he was a surgeon who I had to bail out on several occasions when he got into surgical operations he could not handle. I was introduced to facial fractures. I operated with one of two dentists quite often. I think the results were pretty good, but remuneration was poor. The dentist was paid twice my rate despite being less qualified. One day as I was arriving back from holiday coming through the front door I heard the telephone ringing. There was another facial fracture to be fixed. I got home 20 hours later just in time to start an office. The patient was not insured so all that work was pro bono.

The brightest thing from Bermuda was that I met and married my operating room nurse who is the light of my life. Funnily enough we both trained in Edinburgh at the same time in the same hospitals but never met until Bermuda. Wonderful days sailing with her around the Isles of Bermuda, sun soaked halcyon leisurely blissful enjoyment. I also enjoyed having some influence in the upbringing of her two sons. We lived in a house on the ocean with a swimming pool. To have breakfast on the balcony seeing the waves crash over the rocks was magical. There was a vogue for non-Bermudians to marry Bermudians or those with status for the purposes of staying on the island. . I would never do this. The downside or rather downsides of Bermuda were several. Money was the religion and everything equated to money. Living on the 'rock' was stultifying and to get off was necessary. I used the excuse to attend several conferences and symposia in the USA. l I visited many states all over the country both east and west coasts and south. We also had a house in New Hampshire for our vacations.

I rented a property on Point Finger Road which is the hospital road. This meant visiting patients and working in the hospital was easy. I also set up a small operating room where cosmetic surgery was performed. The powers that be tried to shut me down because we were not using the main hospital but as operating time there was in so short supply I felt it was necessary. I was also the President of the Bermuda Medical Society and as such was in the media on a weekly basis, in the newspapers, radio and television complaining that our remuneration via the insurance companies was being withheld. It did not make me very popular with them.

One of my patients who had flown in from Kenya required urgent surgery to her sinuses which I did in my normal fashion and cured her. There are two operations which were supposed to alleviate the problems, I did the simpler of them but my colleagues in London, who by the way I had lectured to, said I had not done what I said I had because I had not done the different operation that they did. In fact their operation is in my mind dangerous and more extensive than necessary and takes 2 hours whereas mine takes 10 minutes. The results are identical. Now the fashion for the operation is changing back to more of what I did and is termed minimally invasive sinus surgery. The patient laid a complaint with the Bermuda Licensing Board, the General Medical Council in London and the police in Bermuda. The white collar crime unit investigated but thankfully the procurator fiscal had some sense and the whole situation was dropped. I did not trust the police as being a white expat meant I was bottom of the totem pole and my rights were non-existent. In the meantime my immediate colleagues wrote to immigration to say they did not want me, I think because of jealousy as I did operations they were incapable of and my work permit was not renewed. The result was they had to send patients to the USA at huge extra cost. The excuse that my work permit was not renewed was that there were too many ENT surgeons on the Islands. There were three. In fact in the UK there are about 1 ENT for 60,00 people but there are a huge number of junior staff to do most of the work. In Sweden there is 1 ENT surgeon for 20,000 people which is the ratio Bermuda needs given that there are no junior staff. The Minister of Immigration was misled by my immediate colleagues. That was the last time I will help out when the island was about to have no ENT surgeon. That is the thanks I got. At the time my wife had two children on the island and with great soul-searching and tears we left for Canada where one of the boys was at school. My wife was extremely upset at having to leave her sons behind in Bermuda and even to this day she has a lot of self recrimination. She refuses to be an expat again having given 25 years of her life to Bermuda to be kicked in the teeth. She was refused a permanent resident certificate because she was one year shy of the required time of residence. This has now changed in view of the calamitous drop in the work bearing age group of expats. The government seemed to think they could attract workers from all over the world but why would a top executive come to an island where they could only have 1 car and otherwise have to come to work on a motor scooter and pay extortionate rents. Ownership of property was unfairly difficult for expats. The government was wrong and now are trying to rectify the situation, but the proportion of non working islanders is creeping up to 40%.

There are three stories I would like to recall. One day I was trying to moor my boat on a buoy when I misjudged and overran when suddenly the boat stopped. I cut the engine and realised I had tangled the rope of the pennant of a buoy around the propeller of my boat. It took me a few seconds to work out what had happened. There was nothing for it, I stripped down to my boxer shorts and went overboard. I managed to unwind the rope with some difficulty and held the boat in one hand and the buoy rope in the other. The wind got up pushing the boat away from me and I had to stretch like crazy to keep hold of both the boat and the rope. Eventually I managed to get back on the boat and tied a rope onto the buoy. I then rowed back to shore in my skiff, got dressed and went up the overlooking dinghy club. There I met two of my crew members convulsed with laughter at my exploits.

"Thank you very much, why didn't you come to help me?"

In between snorting the reply was "It might have been raining!"

Another morning I went into my office to begin the day's work when I noticed an envelope addressed to me on my desk. I opened it and read

Government offices
Church Street
Hamilton
Telephone 441 293 2727

"Dear Dr Murray,

It has come to our attention that you have moved from Paget to Tuckers Town but we do not have a note of the relocation permit. As you are here under a work permit we regard this as a very serious matter and puts your work permit at risk. Please call me as soon as possible.

Yours truly
C. Lyon.

So I thought not another bloody form to fill in. I'd better sort this out before I start seeing patients. I called the number.

"Hello, this is the aquarium."

"Sorry I must have the wrong number>"

I'll try again and rang the number.

"Hello, the Bermuda aquarium.'

"Could I speak to Mr C, Lyon," I asked.

"Sir, do you know the date today?"

"No, what is the date?"

"April first."

It dawned on me that the perpetrator of this crime was a certain anaesthetist who was playing a joke on me and had removed himself from my ire by disappearing to New York.

My last reminiscence was sailing with my son coming into the dock when the engine of my boat cut out spontaneously. I went past the dock turned the boat dropped the sails and glided into the dock. I shouted to him to jump on the dock with a rope to hold the boat. Unfortunately he only put one foot on the dock the other on the boat. The wind picked up and moved the boat away from the dock, with his legs splaying wider and wider. Thankfully he jumped onto the dock and held the boat to allow us to tie up. Learning by mistakes was my motto regarding sailing.

CHAPTER 12

Canada and wine

It all began when one day in Bermuda I encountered a Canadian who besides his ailment wanted to discuss the predicament of the Canadian economy. On that day the Canadian dollar was only worth 57 cents of the American dollar. "The economy is finished."

As he left my consulting room my mind started racing. Bermuda was fine but I felt there was no future long-term in Bermuda as my work permit had not been renewed and I felt I was working on borrowed time. I felt very vulnerable to be at the behest of the left-wing black government who did not like ex-pats at the best of times. I developed a sinister feeling of insecurity and wanted to develop roots in the country I could depend on. Hence Canada. It so happened that my stepson was at a boarding school in Nova Scotia, so my wife and I took a trip there within one week of hearing the economy woes. Packing up and leaving good friends was very painful and in particular my wife had to leave one son in Bermuda until he became of age to go to boarding school in Canada. We bought a house in Nova Scotia in the November when the Canadian dollar had risen to $.62 US; the Bermuda dollar was on a par with the American dollar so the cost was almost half-price. This all went without a hitch and my wife and I looked forward to the next stage of our lives.

Moving to Canada was not all that easy. To work I had to get a work permit. The rules are that this could not be issued within the country. We set off to get to the nearest foreign country, America. This meant driving to Maine. When we reached St Stephens at the border we crossed over a bridge to be met by the American customs officers."Why do you want to come to the USA?"

"We have to pick up a work permit outside Canada."

"Just go back over the bridge, you don't need to enter USA."

Which is exactly what we did and picked up the work permit at the immigration office. I can't get my head round why we had to jump through these hoops. If we did not get the permit the rules again stated we had to leave Canada every 6 months, why. The reason escapes me.

Eventually we gained Canadian citizenship giving us the same rights as those born in Canada.

The local town is called Wolfville, a university population of 4,500 and the same for the town. The university has several undergraduate courses and some masters courses. Sports are high on the agenda. Although we had saved enough money to retire at the age of 51 after two weeks I was getting very frustrated. I had been between jobs only once before in my life and I was still too young to sit back. I still had something to prove to myself. My perception was that the burgeoning industry in Nova Scotia was wine. It was a difficult concept to get my head round. The weather seemed quite contrary to growing grapes. The thermometers went down to -20°C regularly during winter. Surely grapes are grown in warm climes. Nevertheless there seemed to be at least two wineries functioning and I asked myself if that was what I going to do. I had been a surgeon for 30 years and was reluctant to start a career in surgery in a new country. The rules and regulations were hindrances but more importantly with increasing age I developed a mild tremor and I felt I could not deliver as I used to. So rather than dragging on in misery and possibly cause complications I stopped surgery. In retrospect I felt several of my erstwhile colleagues should have done the same. Also the incumbent ENT surgeons did not want rivalry.

I began to look for suitable land to grow grapes. There did not seem to be an abundance of potential vineyards. At various wineries I was given advice "growing grapes is easy with the fruit at waist level and once the grapes get hold it is difficult to get rid of them. "Just like weeds," said the owner of the nearby winery.

"You need a South facing slope," said another winery owner.

"Why's that?" I questioned.

"Because with the marginal temperatures we get here you want the cold air which is denser to roll down the hill and behind it pull down the warm air from about 40 feet above to warm the grapes to allow ripening."

"Okay" I said to myself "at least I know what I'm looking for."

"What do you do when you drive away every morning and don't return until evening?" Asked my wife.

"I'm driving around to find suitable land for a vineyard. It so happens that after two weeks I may have found the very place," I replied.

"You'd better tell the realtor to find out about more," said my wife.

"I don't know the property you are talking about," said the realtor. "Where in the paper did you see it advertised?"

So the realtor and I arranged to visit. Yes it was a South facing slope but quite a lot of trees, a broken down barn and a three bedroom house in a state of disrepair. We looked at the property in the middle of a snowstorm and when we got to the top of the hill we thought that was the border of the property.

"What size is it?" I asked.

"The realtor for the vendor listed at plus or minus 47 acres." Said the realtor.

"I don't know what that looks like that I think 47 acres is a bit bigger than the area we walked," I said.

The realtor went back to his office and found the details of the property.

"The property extends to about double of what we walked so it extends to the far side of the line of trees we saw towards the east."

"That's better," I said. "Now what are we going to bid?"

"That is the asking price but you could get it for less," said the realtor.

"I'll think about it," I said. The next day I got a phone call from the realtor.

"If you're still interested on the property you have to move on it quickly. They set the closing date for the end of the week and one of my realtor colleagues says his clients will be putting in a very competitive bid. What do you say?"

"Okay I assume that means their bid will be asking price. What about putting in $50 more?" I said.

"Okay sign a formal offer and we'll see," said the realtor. "So be it. I'll let you know what happens on Friday,"

Friday came and almost went until 4:50 when my phone rang.

"You got it!" Congratulated the realtor over the phone. "Come in on Monday and we'll do the paperwork but well done."

So far all had been an idea. I had absolutely no experience of farming and I wondered what was getting into. I did visit the Department of Agriculture which proved to be a particularly useless visit. I was dumbfounded to realize there was no printed advice about how to plant a vineyard; nothing about the types of plants, nothing about sighting of the vineyard, nothing about machinery needed and most of all nothing about the rules and regulations of establishing a vineyard with traffic flow, and clearing forests. In short I found myself on my own with no guidance. I read every book I could find about vineyard husbandry but still my head was buzzing with no action plan coming forth. The immediate problem was to clear the land. Having failed to glean advice from experts I resorted to asking farm machinery outlets. Of course I realized they would sell me anything but in the absence of anything better I was persuaded to buy some basic machinery.

"You want a tractor. What size do you think?" Asked the salesman.

"I don't know. I have about 25 acres of neglected farmland, the rest is trees," I said.

"Okay so this model will be about right. What about a blade for tilling the land, front-end loader and a bush hog for cutting down long grass and bushes? You can go on and on but that should be at least getting you started," said the salesman.

"Okay" I said reluctantly seeing my budget going up in smoke not realizing all that was necessary.

"We'll deliver next week, now what is the address and how we going to pay for this?"

In due course the tractor was delivered. I had never even set in a tractor before. The seat seemed very high off the ground. Nevertheless I was delighted to try and I rode the tractor up and down the hill until after about 20 minutes the tractor cut out. I was not technically minded but I knew enough to check the fuel gauge and make sure all the wires and leads were intact and attached. Nonplussed I called the dealer. The next day a mechanic arrived and checked over the machine. Everything seemed to be working apart from the tractor getting started. The mechanic was just about to go home when as a last resort he removed the cap of the diesel tank and found it empty. The fuel gauge was wrong. So the tractor was picked up and returned to the machinery outlet to be fixed. A few days later the tractor was returned and the bush hog set to work clearing the invasive grass. 10 minutes later several pings emanated from the bush hog followed by a very ugly noise. Again the mechanic was summoned to find several nuts and bolts missing from the bush hog. I was told in future to tighten all the nuts and bolts before using any machinery on every occasion. Indeed the learning curve was steep. Not being used to the cold or agricultural work my work day was shortened to about five hours and after that I went home exhausted. Weeds seemed to grow overnight and the grass was so long even when I sat on the tractor I was dwarfed. There were some apple trees on the property and some Saskatoon berries. I was so ignorant of agriculture I had no idea the apple trees needed to be sprayed several times a year with the result that all became infected with fungus and over a few years died off. Hence the beginning of clearing the land. After six months of trying to clear the land a knight in shining armour appeared in the form of an agricultural worker. He and his wife were looking for accommodation and agreed to clear the land. He was excellent at chainsaw work and many trees were removed. It is much more troublesome to remove the stumps and I had to hire a company to clear up a lot of the roots. At the time I felt lost so I hired an agricultural consultant. This was not helpful as he failed to identify the water drainage of the property. This was very frustrating as I did not see things going the way I wanted. There was an old barn on the property which was structurally unsafe and local kids had to be warned off in case they came to grief if it all fell down. The barn was then removed. Progress stopped in winter with a total cessation of work and in time spring came upon the land heralding new growth, new birds, and new animal tracks like raccoons, foxes and deer. But progress remained slow .At the time another property came on the market. It consisted of a house, a cottage, a very large barn and another falling down barn with about 35 acres of old fruit trees. My mind started thinking that this could be a winery especially as it was situated near the main highway to be able to attract tourists. The house was in a deplorable state, full of what euphemistically could be called junk. The cottage needed a lot of TLC (tender loving care) and the land likewise. The property had been neglected for five years and it showed. Still there was nothing like a challenge. The junk was removed from the house and over the upcoming winter the interior was redesigned. Bedroom walls were broken down, and the internal staircase moved. In fact the whole of the interior was renovated and a conference room was made with a tearoom, kitchen and two other large rooms. The fruit trees all died and my wife and I planted 1000 apple trees in their place. A Herculean effort over three days with subsequent failure of them all within a year. My thoughts were that these things were sent to try us so rather than get disappointed this resulted more strongly than ever to make the project work. For the vineyard to work the undulations of the property needed to be flattened and the damp spots needed to be tile drained. These latter were large perforated plastic tubes buried about 2 feet below the surface to take excess water away. Prior to this my wandering through the farm resulted in getting stuck with the tractor sinking up to the depth of the axles. I had to request the neighbouring farmer with a bigger tractor to pull me out. Once a tile drain had been inserted the ground became firm, what a difference! I had been cynical about the worth of the tile drains but no more. I felt I had to concentrate on this new property and put in a lot of effort to prepare the land to flatten it.. I found the pH of the soil was about 5.6 whereas grapes prefer a pH of 6.8 so I got a contractor to lime the fields .I also attended courses to learn as much as possible about the agriculture but nevertheless did not feel confident particularly after the disaster of the fruit trees. The advice I sought was sometimes good, sometimes bad and often malevolent. Not knowing very much about the whole subject I felt obliged to follow it.. Vines were planted with straight rows. I bought a backhoe to dig ditches to plant some tile drains but progress was very slow and it took several times longer than predicted although by the time a week had gone past I became quite a dab hand at operating the backhoe. Once that had been achieved end posts were sunk into the ground, except at the end of one field a bed of slate needed to be breached to allow the posts to be put in enough to ensure stability. A jackhammer was needed and again a significant time was wasted before the requisite depth could be achieved. Eventually most of the 35 acres were planted with a variety of grapes.

Nova Scotia is cold in the winter. -20°C is quite common in with the wind chill it can get considerably colder. During the first winter myself and the worker were felling very large pine trees in knee deep snow with ambient temperature of -20°C and the wind chill of another 20°C giving a total temperature of -40°C. I previously lived in Bermuda with considerably more temperate weather and in fact when I arrived in Canada I did not have a pair of socks. I was totally unprepared for the bitter Canadian winter. Despite wearing six layers of clothes I was frozen and any inadvertent bare skin was rewarded as if a knife was going in. I could not believe humans could live in such a climate. As a result of the climate normal grapes could not ripen, so the grapes grown in Nova Scotia are artificially made. They are hybrids. The first hybrids were made in the early 1900s by a gentleman by the name of Eugene Kuhlman who is regarded as the father of hybrids. He made several different hybrids most of them somewhat related. These hybrids can withstand temperatures of down to -23 Centigrade.

I hired a crew and 14 acres were planted with a variety of these grapes. I found it frustrating that it took four years before I could get a reasonable harvest but in the meantime the grapes needed to be kept weed free and mould free by spraying. At last those four years were up and the harvest was brought in. The wine making process is complex and took a lot of planning. Firstly we needed collection bins for the grapes. These are plastic about 4 cubic feet. The collected grapes were transported from the fields in much smaller plastic containers which are dumped into the bigger containers. Sometimes the grapes were left to macerate with the weight of the grapes particularly for the red wines to allow the skins to impart colour and taste but for the whites the grapes are immediately put through a crusher destemmer separating the grapes from the stalks. Then the juices were transferred to very large fermentation vats and anointed with yeast. There are various types of yeast depending on what the wine maker wants the wine to taste like. Once fermentation is complete the juices were transferred to bottles. For all this I depended on advice from so-called experts. Some of this advice is good, some not so. Labour was expensive and the harvesting was labour-intensive. So I researched for an automatic harvester and found a second hand one which we christened Matilda. This was a bit rough on the vines but we were amazed at the speed of the harvest. To get a good harvest the vines had to be stressed. My theory is that all living things including humans produce more offspring when stressed. It is well known that humans in distress produce more babies, the affluent middle classes have less children than poor people.

So eventually I had a harvest, modest but a start. I opened the winery to a fanfare with about 50 to 60 people attending. Initially it was quite successful, curiosity being the main attraction. The winemaker was good and the wine sold relatively well. This was followed by the inevitable drop in sales and to stimulate interest I put on free tours of the Vineyard. I enjoyed doing these and was quite used to lecturing in my job as a Senior Lecturer and surgeon. The Greek word for teacher is iatros from which the word iatrogenic comes from, a common term in medicine. Indeed every medical student takes the Hippocratic Oath promising to teach. During the tour I informed my audience that the taste of the grapes depended on several factors which may not be obvious. Firstly terroir means the influence of the soil, location and weather. A lot depends on the individual taster, mood, food recently eaten, and the personality. Regrettably so-called wine experts between themselves vary considerably in their opinions. To my mind if the taster enjoys the wine it is good no matter what someone else's thoughts are.

As it so happened early in the 20 century the previous owner lived in a cottage on the property. He had a still to make hooch. The local police knew this and raided the farm from time to time. Thankfully for the owner there were four exits from the farm allowing his escape to the frustration of the police.

Staff and bureaucracy.

Not all went swimmingly smoothly in the setting up the winery and at times I wondered if I was doing the right thing. My first inklings were when I applied for a license to open the winery. I called the Nova Scotia licensing commission (NSLC) to inquire how to approach this.

"No" I was told after being on the phone for half an hour. "No we don't do this, it is the alcohol tobacco and firearms department to do it."

"Okay," said I said and proceeded to contact the relevant person. Again a prolonged wait over the phone only to be told "no it is the NSLC that do it."

"But they told me you do it," I replied in exasperation.

"Who told you that?" Asked the ATF spokesperson.

I gave the NSLC's representative's name and was told the NSLC spokesperson should know better. There were rules and rules and rules. At times I felt I should have to ask permission to pass gas!

There was a rickety barn on the property that was in a dangerous situation. It was three stories high and filled with excrement from hens and mice as well as rotten wood. I wanted it removed before it fell down and injured someone. At the time I was playing host to the local farmers market over the winter and found it difficult to keep visitors out of the barn. I found somebody who wanted the wood so I suggested he take it. While doing this the barn collapsed, thankfully with no one in it.

"How can you justify the cost of the license for the winery when you don't do anything for it," I inquired of the county planners.

"That's the cost. We don't have to justify it," was the reply.

One day the NSLC representative showed up to inspect the potential winery. By that stage I had not formulated all my plans but was strongly warned that this lady was the queen of licensing and if she did not approve there would be no winery. I wanted a telegraph pole moved to a less obstructive site. Another license of $1000 and the cost of moving it.. Some electrical work was needed to be relocated. Another license. Then the waste from the winery needed attention. After much coming and froing a sewage system was put in place. I later discovered the system was far too large for the winery and I felt I had been conned. Not only was that but the money I paid for the system was pocketed by the contractor so the license was not granted until this money was handed over to the appropriate authority. I wanted a pond at the bottom of the property opened up by Ducks Unlimited. Again a special license was needed to ensure any waterways would not be compromised. Headache after headache. There were constant licenses needing to be obtained, all of which utilized several members of staff at a high cost. All this was before a penny was made selling the wine. That meant further bureaucracy. I wondered how many wineries got off the ground. There were hurdles at every turn. By this time I had had the house converted into a small restaurant with other potential meeting rooms. I also put up a tent to accommodate weddings, dances etc. I found I needed a license to sell alcohol in the house but a different license from a different licensing body to allow alcohol sales in the tent which was all of 10 yards away. Whenever I wanted to put on a dance another license was required as well as paying dues to the musicians Union. It seemed overwhelming. Nearing the end of my tether the signage became a real problem. The rules in Kings County are strict. After creating a sign on the main highway indicating the winery was 400 yards down a side road I was told this was illegal. I pointed out many, many other transgressions in the county. The administration were not interested in these only mine. I was threatened with prosecution but by this stage I was absolutely sick of the whole business and owing to the accumulation of coincident setbacks I decided to sell the winery. There's a phrase taken from the sailing fraternity "the happiest day in a sailor's life is when he buys his boat. And an even happier day is when he sells it."

Staff

As a surgeon I was used to having orders followed and I made the mistake of naïvely thinking Nova Scotians would do the same. Not so. At first with the land clearing and simple tasks I employed local labour who were paid are as regular contractors. There were some minor infractions but basically everything ticked along. Then with advice the first vineyard was planted. Wide experience of vineyard husbandry was suggested and lacking in contacts I accepted this advice. Initially the vineyard took shape with further planting and spraying and all the other necessities. It was suggested planting different varieties of grapes. All went well for about three years although even at that relatively early stage I was beginning to become suspicious as this advice became suspect. I was persuaded that all the new vines needed to be grafted which was not needed. This meant having to employ more staff In winter whereas normally they would be laid off. In Canada seasonal workers wages are made up when laid off from Employment Insurance. Money from the employer is paid over to this organization as well as some money from the worker. The employer also paid tax for the privilege of employing someone. I find this incomprehensible. Here was a province with one of the highest unemployment rates in the country, the highest taxes and they punish employers. No wonder more businesses employ part-time as opposed to full-time workers when they do not have these ongoing burdens. The agricultural team during the summer harvested cuttings from existing vines for the next year's propagation. I was not sure but I felt that on purpose some vines were being mixed up and I did not realize that was the case until four years later when I found different grapes grew in the same row. When the operation grew and more workers especially students were needed things became worse. One student using an auger to make a hole in the ground for plants was overheard to say "if I break this auger I will not have to work it.". Mould was left to destroy many of the vines. Another worker planted end-posts in a very higgledy-piggledy fashion. I think my lack of respect in my staff was mutual. However a lesson I learned, I could not walk on water and in life it is better to stick to what you know. I was very disappointed with the workers of Nova Scotia and vowed never to employ anybody again in the province.

The learning curve was very steep and despite asking many people I did not get a lot of help. Grapevines require a trellis to grow and support them. In fact we had a tree on the property which served that purpose for grapes the original nature's way. From my reading I learned grapes were thought to begin their existence in Mesopotamia (Iraq and Kuwait) in 10,000 BC. The demigod ruler at the time was Gilgamesh. At each end of a row some sort of anchor was needed. Again with advice the easiest method was to use the metallic rims of car tires at a depth of 3 feet and laid flat. This entailed a visit to a local junkyard to hunt between the masses of discarded metal ware. Wire was attached to these rims and strung along attached to the wooden end posts and extended attached to small metal posts to the other wooden end post. The rows should not be too long as the wind may make them blow out like a sail. They should be north south facing to achieve maximum sunlight. We planted roses at each end of the rows. This was to detect mould before it showed up on the vines. I think it was just as well I still had enthusiasm and energy at that time. It was hard work. As the winery matured so did tourism. I took groups around the vineyard and I hope I gave them an informative talk. This reminded me of my time as a senior lecturer in Edinburgh University. I would walk into the lecture theatre and ask for the topic of the lecture was. Once I knew that I went into an automatic mode reiterating all my knowledge on that subject.

One of the areas we planted was flat. While putting in the tile drains I encountered a flatbed of shale which made the tile drains difficult to dig in the usual 2 feet. This slowed progress considerably. I subsequently learned that during the Ice Age a glacier had moved the topsoil from that flat area and deposited across a stream to make a hill, otherwise called a drumlin. This was all second hand knowledge and I was a bit wary about delivering all these facts not knowing who I was talking to. In fact on one occasion two geologists came to me afterwards to agree that drumlin was the correct word. "Phew."

The result was that the grapes grown on the flat tasted somewhat flinty compared with the same grapes grown on the hill. It takes four years for the vines to produce a decent crop, a frustrating time. In the meantime there are predators to take care of. Deer like to eat the leaves of the vines so we discourage them by suspending soap around the periphery, the smell kept them away. They also did not like hot spicy substances under their feet. Birds are very clever creatures and they sensed when the grapes ripened. This coincided with the advent of fall so by nature they wanted to stock up for the winter. The traditional way to keep them at bay was netting. This is expensive not only on the nets but the labour required. There are a variety of balloons, flags, tinsel and other windblown techniques to frighten birds but they get used to them. Sudden loud noises do make them fly but they just settled down again and after a while they realize the noise is not threatening. Our attempt at noise protection merely brought a complaint from a neighbour with a visit from the police. In fact the noise came from a nearby winery. I think I confused the policeman by quoting the law that in Nova Scotia I had the 'right to farm'. Perhaps the best was the bird of prey, the falcon. We hired a falconer with his trained bird to scare the starlings. This worked for four days after the visit but again the birds returned. There are some model Falcons which are said to frighten the starlings and robins but I could not get hold of some. Another predator was raccoons. These are ubiquitous in Nova Scotia. Dogs can be trained to fight and kill them with variable success but trapping is the best. I joke when I say we take the trapped Raccoons to a neighbouring winery and release them there. The last predator is the airborne louse phylloxera. These bury into the roots of the vine thereby killing it. It was very prevalent in Europe in the 1880s and more or less decimated the wine industry. It was noted that Californian vines were resistant and the rootstock was taken from there and replanted in Europe. The result was a renaissance of the European wine industry..

But it was incredibly frustrating. When I first started growing grapes no one give me any advice so I learned this from trial and error. Also the people I employed as advisors were less than truthful.

For instance the most popular grapes grown in Nova Scotia are called L'Acadie Blanc. They are hybrids which have a natural resistance to phylloxera but I was told they had to be grafted onto it stop to prevent infestation. That was just one of big lies in an effort to create unnecessary work. I just do not understand the short sightedness when if I got co-operation the winery would have been more successful and more money would be available for better wages.

During the tours I encouraged visitors to ask questions. I explained that I learned from these questions and said that this business is like medicine, as soon as you think you know everything something new crops up and if you stop learning it is time to pack it up.

"What grapes do you grow here," asked an interested wine expert or an oenophile.

"All of our grapes are hybrids. They are man-made to be able to be harvested in our relatively short summer season. A good wine has a balance of sugar and acid to give it that bite so our L'Acadie Blanc retains that oomph factor. In fact L'Acadie is very malleable, it can be made dry, sweet, sparkling or any variation. It depends on the winemaker. It grows well here which is about 45° latitude, the same as Bordeaux but without the Gulfstream for warmth. The one thing I do not understand is that here in Annapolis Valley the mean temperature is better than the Atlantic Coast, possibly because of the closeness of the Ocean and resulting fogs."

"I see you have bees on the property, are they good for pollinating the grapes?" Asked another interested party.

"No, grapes do not need the pollination, they have male and female components to give self-pollination. Each cluster of grapes needs 14 leaves to gain enough sunlight to ripen and it takes roughly 2 plants to make one bottle of wine."

"Where do the names of the grapes come from?" Inquired another visitor.

"The grandfather of grape hybrids was a gentleman called

Eugene Kuhlman who pioneered their production. He began in the early 20th century and produced several cousins of grapes calling them after prominent citizens. There is Leon Millot who was a world traveller at the time, Marechal Foch and Marechal Joffre who signed the armistice in 1918 and Lucy Kuhlman who was the daughter of Eugene. We also grow L'Acadie Blanc and Sauvignon Blanc. L'Acadie is a hybrid originally made in Ontario but because the climate is warmer than here it ripened too early and the acid fell out giving a bland wine whereas here the climate is ideal. We have a small number of less popular grapes. By the way I'm sure you have been told that grapes can only grow on south facing slopes in Nova Scotia. We grow Sauvignon Blanc on north facing slopes."

"How did you start, did you buy in small plants?"

"No I went to a local vineyard and with the owner's permission picked up the prunings and planted these into the ground, quite simple really with a fairly good take rate. I'll tell you our first exposure to a vineyard. We had just arrived from Bermuda and I was interested in getting into the grape industry, something quite different from my previous career. A realtor suggested visiting a small vineyard about 30 minutes away. It was April but snow was still lying. We were introduced to a small Portuguese man who lived a day's journey away. He worked on the vineyard staying in a caravan during the week and went back to New Brunswick at the weekend. His accent was very strong and it was difficult to make him out. We trudged through knee-deep snow which slopped over our Wellington boots to try to see the vines. He was an expert in concrete and had made his in posts of concrete. The rows seemed higgledy-piggledy and not all the plants looked the same. At the end of the tour he insisted we take a bottle of red and a bottle of white wine home for our 'supre'. Later that day we tasted the wine, it tasted of diesel and despite our ability to drink almost anything alcoholic, the wine was quite undrinkable. I hope you find our wines drinkable so please try some gratis. This is unlike all the other wineries which charge for tasting."

So ended the tour, I hoped the free tour would increase business. That was a problem. The winery was off the main road by about 400 m so how to attract passing trade? The answer was to put up a sign on the main highway directing traffic our way. So we put up a very interesting wooden sign on a neighbour's property in exchange for a case of wine every year. This caused a lot of excitement in the provincial offices.

"You have to get permission to put up a sign," I was told.

"Why what difference does it make to you?" I replied.

"The bylaws of the county say you cannot have that sign."

"Why?"

"It has to be on your property."

"But my neighbour is quite happy to have the sign."

"No, it has to come down."

"What about all the other signs not on properties like in Port Williams. Queens County are happy to help businesses succeed with their off property signage. Why are you so adamant in trying to put me out of business?"

"We had a complaint so the sign must go."

"I can't believe how stupid that is. I think I know who the complainer is, just because I fired him. What's his name?"

"We can't divulge that."

"You mean the complaint from one disgruntled ex-employee can put several other employees out of work, preposterous! Every day in the summer season tourists come in saying that we didn't know you were here, only the sign told us."

A lesson I learned about bureaucracy was 'it is better to beg forgiveness than ask permission'. So I didn't do anything and left the sign up. A few weeks later I had another visit from the bureaucracy.

"If you don't take that sign down we'll take you to court and you will receive a large fine and then we'll take it down," demanded the civil servant.

"What about all the other signs in the province not on the owner's property?"

"That's nothing to do with it."

"Yes it is."

The other bureaucratic problem was that Canada is made up of provinces and territories which are autonomous. This meant we could not export our wine to any other jurisdiction. Crazy.

I wonder to myself why it is it so difficult to do business in this province. You'd think the small minded people do not want to see success on the doorstep. My thoughts went back to when I first came to Canada. Soon after arriving a referendum in Nova Scotia was held to assess the feasibility of stores opening on Sundays. The result – no shopping allowed, everyone goes to church and it is a family day. Hello, not everyone goes to church and for some Sunday was the only day they could go shopping and not everyone had a family. Eventually the government allowed Sunday shopping and it became the busiest shopping day of the week as it has been shown in many other places to be the case. We wondered; this is like Scotland last century when we had to stay behind curtained windows having been to the church to be forgiven for our weekday sins. Perhaps this is why Nova Scotia is not progressing. There was the Ivany report indicating the aging population and diminishing workforce suggesting minimal encouragement from the government to rectify the situation before it becomes a disaster.

"We like the way it is without change" is a common retort from lifelong Nova Scotians. This in my opinion is a very short sighted approach.

Then I come to the problem with Nova Scotian workers. It seems that the workforce is extremely itinerant particularly at the level I needed as workers. There were indeed some stalwarts who gave a good day's work for the wages but all too often there were the skivers. They knew all rules of employment and played them to the fullest extent. At first preparing the land was easy. The workers understood what was necessary but with the disappearance of several tools I began to wonder. At this time I realized that my financial reserves would be totally drained without an injection of dollars. It would take at least four years for the crop to ripen before actually making wine. I decided to become a doctor again. I jumped through the hoops required but at the last hurdle a local ear nose and throat surgeon decided she did not want another surgeon so applied to the Nova Scotia College of physicians and surgeons to prevent me practicing my specialty in Kings County. I could however be a surgeon in Halifax but that was impractical because I lived one hour away. By chance during my spell in Bermuda I had embarked on training in allergy. This involved attending seminars and conferences in several American cities, online learning and culminating in an exam in San Antonio Texas. I then became a Fellow of the American Academy of Otolaryngological Allergists. I set up an allergy practice in Kentville. From my roots I inherited a misunderstanding of the importance of allergies. In my time in undergraduate training allergy was a bit of a joke, not to be taken seriously and I think to some extent this attitude pertains in the United Kingdom. However in North America it is quite different with allergies being very prominent. Perhaps patients' perception is different but ragweed in North America produces a lot of allergy symptoms.

At the beginning stage of the winery we were fairly early on the project so I willingly took advice. Unfortunately I was not well informed and bowed to apparent superior knowledge. The bureaucratic nightmare of becoming a winery was disheartening. Again why are there so many hurdles? Do you not want me to set up a business? But I was misled. Several pieces of equipment disappeared. One example was a distance measuring instrument claiming it was necessary to measure the length of the rows but secretly for assessing the distance to the golf hole. Eventually I had enough and stopped taking advice. Soon after someone broke into the winery after that and stole all the records so that when the time came to look at the finances, I was in total ignorance. I was told that someone tried to get me in trouble with the Winery Association. My attempts to employ better advice was unsuccessful. The advice I was given was disastrous and I wondered if it was just me or was the local talent just not up to the job. Other wineries do not seem to have the same problems. I have been told by numerous ex-pats trying to set up business in Nova Scotia there was a prevalent thought that expats had lots of money and could afford to give it out until there was none left. A bookkeeper despite several requests refused to give me the finances because not all of the bills and expenses had been given to her.

I asked "could you please give me an idea of how we're doing?"

"Can't yet, I will when I get all the info."

Again and again I asked for figures for sales with no answers. Every Monday morning the bank called saying the account was in the red and could I put some money in. Eventually I said 'no more money.' This prompted resignations. There was little respect for equipment which regularly broke down unnecessarily. Another young man seemed to be willing to learn about winemaking. I made him an assistant to our peripatetic Rastafarian winemaker who seem to make reasonable wine but had to go to the bathroom every half hour. I never did understand why. His employment was not renewed to so we depended on an American. He gave good advice although he did make very sweet wines. I sent this young man to the States to learn from him. Having paid his travel board and lodging as well as his wages he resigned one week after coming back. Then there was this traveller who we employed to tend to the vines. He wanted to smoke marijuana on the job so he lasted one and a half hours. There was a dearth of dependable workers. I wanted to employ Mexicans where I had contacts as local farmers employed Mexicans, Jamaicans and Barbadians with apparent ease. With further investigation I realized that I was blocked by my employees who did not want to relinquish the power over the workforce.

One aspect of the job I really hated was the farmer's markets. I felt we needed a high profile in Wolfville and Halifax but I have never experienced such mind bending boredom in my life. My wife enjoyed it much more but in my previous medical jobs the patients came to me; selling wine was quite the opposite.

We thought a nice small restaurant to complement the winery would be beneficial. This involved restoration of the house and initially it was very successful. The chef we had was good and made excellent soups. One day he invited his wife to come for lunch and the next day he wanted a raise in his salary. The restaurant was losing money and I refused his request. He left. We then had a succession of so-called chefs none of which came up to a reasonable standard. At one stage my wife stepped in and took on the job as well as doing my secretarial work and again underlying her loyalty. A lot of kitchen equipment disappeared when a variety of cooks were employed which I was told by other restaurant owners was common in Nova Scotia.

My daughter had travelled to several parts of the world and I thought she would be ideal to inherit the business in due course. Unfortunately she decided that the winery was not for her and left. After all of this I sold the winery and got rid of my headache, thank goodness. In retrospect I let so-called experts run the business when they were at best incompetent and at worse malicious. A good lesson learned. I will never employ anyone again in Canada. The employment law is so slated against the employer to be almost untenable. I suppose I was employing the dross of the work force, but I could not fathom the lack of work ethic. Is this the result of a socialist culture? Overall the winery experience was just that, a learning process about human failings, thankfully we came out of it even but I would not encourage anyone to do it again.

ALLERGY

Early on in the process I realized that this wine business was a lot more expensive than I thought so I tried to start a practice again. I was not allowed to be an ENT surgeon. Coincidently I later developed a Dupytrens contracture in both hands resulting in a crippling condition of unrestrained flexure of the middle and ring fingers making surgery difficult. Subsequent injection and surgery have made day to day use quite practical but operating a scalpel would be difficult. I had trained in allergy in various locations in the USA and was awarded a Fellow in the American Academy of Otolaryngic Allergies, so I began an allergy clinic. It has been stated that if the clinician listens fully the patient will tell him or her the diagnosis. This was borne out in my practice.

For the first time in my career I had to think about the patient's mind and how to help them help themselves. This is in my opinion the crux of good healthcare. The patient these days in Western culture has the knowledge to help themselves with living, feeding, exercise and lifestyle, so the onus rests on them and not the health care professional. I strongly feel financial burdens should be put on those factors that damage health such as mind altering drugs, junk food, tobacco, alcohol and fast cars with gas guzzling. I also feel that over prescribing of antibiotics has resulted in the emergence of resistant super bugs; I predicted this 20 years ago. Of course politicians stop short of encouraging healthy eating because the unpopularity and expense of my diet but perhaps the introduction of a sugar tax is the beginning to persuade people to help themselves. I felt my previous surgical skills were beginning to wane and rather than continue I realized it was time to drop the surgery bit. I wish more surgeons had that insight. I did the usual skin tests of trees, weeds grasses mould, cats,dogs, dust, dust mite and any other unusual indicated tests, but pretty soon it came to me that a lot of the patients symptoms were the result of an awful diet. I asked the patients to write down everything that went through their mouth for 7 days. That was quite a revelation! The junk that people eat was unbelievable. Usually the diary showed over much in the way of carbohydrates, but most patients said that was the cheapest food available on their budget. Fast food is heavily advertised in North America.

I also ran a methadone clinic at the behest of my own general practitioner until his colleagues could qualify in opioid addiction management. . This meant I had to sit my last exam ever. I felt sorry for these poor inadequate easily led patients almost all who apart from opioid abuse used marijuana daily. In those days it was illegal but in the turn of events, Canada has recently legalised the habit. The government stands to make a huge profit from this legalisation.

The overall difference between my experience in the UK and American lifestyles is that in the UK repression is the keyword as opposed to the other side of the pond where encouragement is the norm. In Scotland the phrase "You cannae be ony guid, I kent your faither' is widely held. My philosophy was to go as far as I could in my career and thought there were no no's in my ambitions. I have found that nationalism and racism seem to be more important than talent with natives given priority. This is a contentious problem, but I wonder how many generations does one go back to claim native rights.

I realised I had underestimated the cold of the Canadian winters with small icebergs appearing in the middle of the sea, a new phenomenon for me. We decided that we did not like the cold so we now go to Mexico for the winter. San Miguel de Allende in the state of Guanajuato is a 400 year old city with cobbled streets, a lot of history and many artists. Ten percent of the resident population is North American so it is a bit like home from home. We have made several friends in a dining club and I love playing croquet at I believe the only club in Mexico. We travelled to Laredo on the American Mexico border and got a permanent resident card for Mexico meaning entry to Mexico was a lot easier. Entering America was very strict but returning to Mexico was easy by walking across the bridge over the Rio Grande and no officials to check our credentials.

Having said my working life in medicine had its ups and downs overall I enjoyed it and achieved everything I wanted and would recommend it but the changes in the way health care is organised by various governments to my mind contribute to the low morale suffering by those who work in it. Most health care workers are highly motivated but along with the bullying ethos and low pay the service will not attract the best and the service will suffer. I think many of my shortcomings are the result of eschewing politics particularly in medicine but that is my personality and I make no excuses. I do not like being in the limelight and prefer to be wallpaper. Perhaps also medical school does its best to dehumanise students so at the end we behaved like zombies and the wine business was an opportunity to try something else. On the other hand you can't teach an old dog new tricks. I gave up the medical practice when I was informed I had to appoint a mentor and pay him to check up on me. The reason was I was not a Canadian graduate. As I had practiced my specialty for 40 years I felt quite insulted. Not only did I teach but I happened to examine a local ENT surgeon in his Fellowship for the Royal College of Surgeons in Edinburgh. I have more qualifications than any Nova Scotian ENT surgeons but none of them practiced allergies to my level. So I retired. Having experienced several different health care systems I have found no perfect approach to good health apart from patients' own self responsibility. I fear several governments have succeeded in diminishing public opinion of health care professions in the same manner they have of teaching professions. I would warn budding surgeons that medicine as a whole is a very jealous mistress and I abhor what I see today of working to rule by many of the medical fraternity and not giving their all to the well-being of their patients. Having said all that I think my understanding of the effect of diet on health is my most uplifting discovery of my career.

THE VITALITY DIET

P art of my allergy practice was to try to persuade patients to help themselves by adopting a healthier way of eating. My medical colleagues felt this was not real medicine as they were not taught this at medical school and I was called a charlatan and worse by them. I regret that so called intelligent people should have such closed minds to "new thinking". However the results spoke for themselves. It is a shame these doctors are programmed to prescribe medicines instead of getting to the root problem and encouraging patients to help themselves.

Most diets are just about losing weight quickly, irrespective of the impact on long-term health and wellbeing. This diet is different. My vitality diet is about identifying foods found in modern diets which are causing us to have bowel and skin conditions, reducing our energy and preventing us from living full, happy lives. I have drawn on my experience treating thousands of patients and developed a diet which can be tailored to each individual's needs. Although most patients lose about 10 pounds at the start of the diet, this is a medically-developed eating programme focussed on your body's internal health. So if you want to really get healthy and feel better for it, come start your journey with us.

This project is designed to help control the symptoms of Irritable Bowel Syndrome (IBS). The culprits seem to be a combination of sugars and yeast in the diet. There may be alleviation of other symptoms as a side effect of the treatment. The approach is totally natural but requires the person to apply themselves to the food plan which is not easy and some people cannot manage the will power needed. It is essential that medical input is incorporated especially if diabetes is present as there may be a precipitous decrease in blood sugar.

ANATOMY

The gastrointestinal tract begins at the mouth and ends at the anus. Food and drink passes from the mouth down the oesophagus into the stomach where the milieu is extremely acidic with hydrochloric acid. The acidity may render probiotics, used for IBS, useless. Next lies the duodenum where bile from the gall bladder neutralizes the acidity. The food continues through the jejunum. The duodenum and the jejunum are collectively called the small intestine. Lining the small intestine are multiple projecting fronds called villi. These increase the surface area to make more absorption of nutrients. In gluten enteropathy these villi are absent giving rise to malabsorption. The food then enters the large intestine which includes firstly the caecum, from which buds the appendix, then the ascending colon followed by the transverse, descending colon and eventually the rectum and finally the anus. It is thought that IBS occurs mainly in the large intestine.

Pathology

The large intestine contains multiple trillions of microorganisms including yeast. It is thought that when the balance of these organisms is upset IBS occurs. IBS is characterized by either diarrhea or constipation with associated abdominal bloating. There may be other symptoms. The severity of the IBS symptoms is very subjective: the level of complaints depends on the personality of the sufferer.

When there is an overgrowth of yeast in the large intestine or excess in the diet the balance previously referred to is upset. Other causes include antibiotics and mouthwashes, which kill off good bacteria, and excess sugar ingestion. Substances called lectins are present in many foods. There are good and bad lectins. These bad lectins are contained in many foods and in particular in soy and wheat. These bad lectins combine with sugar molecules in the large intestine and attach to the lining cells of the colon. In turn these cells lose their attachment to each other, i.e. lose their 'tight junctions', and allow the colon contents through the protection of the lining cells allowing the formation of a 'leaky gut syndrome'. It is theorized yeast and other toxic colonic contents enter the blood stream and circulate around the body. These proteins are recognized as foreign and stimulate an allergic reaction.

HOW THE DIET WORKS

The Nuts and Bolts

The object of the program is to restrict the ingestion of yeast and carbohydrate which become sugars. In the past I prescribed all sorts of supplements in the form of vitamins and oils but now I know these are not needed. The body can sort itself out. It may take several weeks but if the recommendations are followed there is almost 100% success rate. If however the patient's focus is lost the symptoms may return after some time so this diet becomes a life style of eating. I cannot emphasize enough this is NOT a quick fix. Initially the change in eating habits is challenging particularly in the first two weeks. This is made worse in some people by the die off of yeast in the body, the Herxheimer Reaction, which produces 'flu like symptoms in about two weeks after the start of the program. These symptoms last about 24 hours and then the weight starts to come off and the energy increases.

It is essential that other causes of bowel upset are excluded before embarking on these recommendations namely cancer, ulcerative colitis, diverticular disease, Crohn's disease and others.

A side effect of the program is weight loss of up to 10lbs in the first month. The weight loss slows down in subsequent months. If there is not a significant weight loss in the first month the food and drink ingested should be re-examined with another food diary. A list of suitable recipes can be found at THEVITALITYDIET.com.

Having fully retired from both the medical and wine business I could now start on my bucket list.

MY RETIREMENT ADVENTURES..

Trans-Siberian Railway reflections.
Here I am sitting in the middle of Mongolia fulfilling a childhood dream. The snow is all-encompassing and sparkling under the midday sun which is partially obscured by clouds. Pine trees abound on the steep slopes of the surrounding mountains. The occasional semi-stray dog breaks the white quilt but otherwise there is no sign of the local fauna.

It all started as a child, I've always been fascinated by railways and in particular ones that traverse large chunks of the globe including cultures and climates. I really have no idea what it entailed and as the travel agent said this was a learning process for both her and me.

What about the trans-Siberian railway? Why is it so alluring? From as long as I remember I have wanted to go on this railway, the longest in the world at 9,289 kilometers first built from 1891 to 1916. This was from Moscow to Vladivostok but the route I took branched off at Irkusk the capital of Siberia to end in Beijing, China. I have always liked railways and this would constitute another box to be ticked like the time I ran a marathon and also trekked in Nepal. I cannot explain but perhaps it could be likened to climbing a mountain because it's there. After retirement my wife said "do it now while you can." So with a degree of trepidation excitement and curiosity I booked the trip. The price was very reasonable and I did not want to go on a private train but rather meet the natives and find out more about the culture of the countries I visited. I often thought about doing the luxury train but you are stuck with likeminded passengers and do not have the opportunity to meet the people of the country quite apart from the price difference which was at least 3 times the cost of my trip. Preparations began several months prior with applications for visas for both Russia and China but for some reason Canadians did not need a visa for Mongolia although EU residents did.

I visited in November thinking the weather would be cool but did not appreciate this was a gross underestimate. I flew from Halifax Nova Scotia to Heathrow London and after realizing the next president of the USA was the shock choice of the American public boarded an Aeroflot liner to Moscow. It all went very smoothly until we got to the inevitable lineup at Russian immigration. Not being a very patient man I found it very frustrating to be delayed and almost voiced my opinion as to the holdup but thankfully kept my mouth shut as being in a foreign country one has to obey their rules. Having waited about half an hour for my passport to be stamped, customs was a dawdle and I was met by a lady holding up a placard with my name on it. Extremely efficiently a car delivered me to the four-star hotel I was booked in. Having a morbid fear of heights I was booked in the top story of the 23 story hotel. I should have said something when I booked the trip. It was one of the busiest hotels in the city and one of the most difficult to get attention. For instance I wanted to email my wife but it took at least four attempts to work out how to do this.

The next morning I spotted my next tour guide in the lobby holding up a placard with my name. She was totally fluent in English. She asked me if I had been to Moscow before which I had 25 years previously. So she modified my tour and the first stop particularly as it had been snowing the night before was the Metro. I recalled these underground railway stations were magnificently built with marble walls and chandeliers. I'm told that Stalin wanted to impress the Russian populace of the culture of communism. I am not sure if that was the message received but certainly the architecture is magnificent. Quite the opposite of most Western subways. The whole service was very efficient with trains arriving almost every few minutes. Moscow is said to have a population of about 17 million but unofficially the figure is 21,000,000 with unregistered incomers. The city forefathers had the vision to expand the boundaries of the city with protected undeveloped areas. Statues of Lenin abound but Stalin seems to be persona non grata. After visiting several stations my tour guide and I came to the surface near the Red Square. On the way we passed several magnificent architectural beauties which I appreciated very much. I spotted a man standing on the roof of four storeys shoveling snow and ice down onto the street. Apparently there are several deaths every year from ice falling on unaware pedestrians. This prophylaxis prevented these unnecessary fatalities. Next door is a cathedral. The original destroyed by the antireligious Stalin but was rebuilt in the early 1990s along with a gate into Red Square. The rebuild sought to re-create the original and the inside has been restored in the original concept to look decades older. On the next block we came across GUM the iconic shopping mall. It is pronounced GOOM. When I was there 25 years ago the shelves were bare and the place appeared depressed. Today, what a change! The place glittered with all the top class stores normally found in Harrods of London and Fifth Avenue New York. The transformation was startling and possibly reflective of the change in society several decades after the collapse of communism. We then walked into the adjacent Red Square where they were sectioning off a large skating rink for the winter. As a result I could not get a sight of Lenin's tomb or the other VIPs such as Yuri Gagarin's final resting places in front of the Kremlin walls. However the gates to the Kremlin appeared to be shut and as I had visited inside previously we did not try to enter. I seem to recall the wealth contained within was in consummate contrast to the concept of communism.

The relatively light dusting of snow produced bedlam to the traffic. I was surprised as I would expect a routine to have been worked out decades ago to deal with the inevitable weather. Saint Basil's cathedral, with its iconic multicoloured domes glittering even under the wintry sun, completes the Square. If Stalin had had his way this would have been destroyed but thankfully he was resisted to allow it to go unscathed. Our next stop was the cemetery where those who had fallen out of favor were buried. The most notable is Nikita Sergeyevich Khrushchev whose star began to fall after the disastrous Bay of Pigs fiasco in Cuba when he tried to set up a threat to the USA with rockets pointing north. The artist who made the headstone was hated by Khrushchev but despite this his son commissioned him to design the grave reflecting his black-and-white personality. BorisYelstin is buried under a large sculpture of the Russian flag as his widow felt many have his actions should not be remembered.

A fine example of Moscow Baroque is the Novodevichy convent otherwise known as the New Maiden's Monastery. Within the tall red walls built in the manner of Jerusalem lies the oldest structure, the Solemsky Cathedral built in 1524-1525. The whole area contains many churches. Many ladies from Russian Royal families and Boyar clans were forced to take the veil and lived in the 'nunnery'. It was closed in 1922 by the Bolsheviks but reopened by Stalin as a sop to the Greek Orthodox Church in 1943 as the Moscow Theological Institute and finally in 1994 the nuns returned. It is a UNESCO World Heritage site. Moscow is resplendent with statues mostly depicting either war victories or the success of the workers overcoming the bourgeoisie of the Czarists reign. One such is celebrating the achievements of women but Stalin strongly objected to this and at one stage the artist had to resort to hiding under the skirts of the sculpture to avoid arrest. The model was originally demonstrated in Paris and subsequently was moved permanently to Moscow. We went on to the Cathedral of Christ the Savior. On December 25, 1812 the last soldiers of Napoleon's army left Russia forever. On the same day Emperor Alexander the First signed a royal manifesto on the construction of the Cathedral of Christ the Savior in Moscow to "show our gratitude to divine providence for saving pressure from the destruction that threatened her." The war with Napoleon, known in Russia as the patriotic war of 1812, proved to be a sort of God's warning against the fashion for everything French which had obsessed Russian society since the 18th century. It also arose unprecedented patriotism in all strata of the country's population. After the death of Alexander I his younger brother Nicholas the First continued with the construction. The building is 100 m high and took 44 years to build. The cathedral was exploded on December 5, 1931 at the height of communist rule and the site was turned into an open-air swimming pool. In a way fortunately the subsequent evaporation of steam seriously damaged paintings in the nearby Pushkin Museum of fine arts and the pool was removed so rebuilding of the Cathedral was initiated on January 7, 1995. On August 19, 2000 it was consecrated and it was immediately turned into the major Christian center of the country. Both the interior and exterior are quite magnificent and well worth a visit. Our next port of call was the international space Museum. This was quite a revelation depicting the Soviet race to master outer space. On view is a model of the original Sputnik, then several subsequent models including those rockets carrying dogs and eventually humans. The thing that struck me was the size of these first cosmonauts; tiny. It makes sense to keep the whole structure as light and small as possible. There was also a mockup space station and various models and original rocket satellites and meteors. I think the tour guide's enthusiasm was a reflection of the fact that several of her relatives worked on the space program.

I offered to pay for the Metro and other incidentals but this was refused. Overall I was suitably impressed by Moscow.

THE SIBERIAN TRAIN

In true Russian spirit my place on the train was impersonally named number two carriage nine berth 19. A host of Russian soldiers flooded the platform. They looked so young and it was hard to believe they are putting their lives on the line for mother Russia. Within each compartment there were four berths arranged in a European style of couchettes with two sleeping on the upper berths and during the day the lower berths were converted into seats. We were issued with clean sheets and pillow covers to last the journey. Blankets were also available. During the day a lot of people slept as the countryside became boring and many dozed so sleep at night was to some extent compromised but the movement and background noise of the train appeared to have a soothing soporific effect and the time spent sleeping was much longer than usual although the quality was less good. It was as if my brain went into suspended animation.

My wife and I had many discussions as to whether she would accompany me. I am so glad we decided against it as she would have hated it. The whole aspect of what I eventually realized was a commuter train was like going back to student days with roughing it, not her style at all. At the end of the carriage was the modern-day samovar producing boiling water day and night. This was in essence a boiler with no fancy decorations. At the other end were the washrooms. Only two for 36 people. Although there was both hot and cold running water there was no shower facilities. I was concerned because my bowels get upset with the change in water from country to country. I took Dukoral to ward off E.Coli poisoning which I suffered many years before. It was most unpleasant with severe abdominal bloating diarrhea and gas. I might also have contracted giardiasis (GEE-ARD-DIE-ASIS) which again is a stomach bug. I must have picked it up on my travels. The result was I had to pass huge quantities of quite objectionable gas. The most embarrassing time was in my private practice as I explained previously. Most embarrassing. After about a year of this with several treatments of Flagyl which was supposed to be a cure I came across a former trainee who was working in Kenya. She recognized the problem immediately as it was common where she worked. The medication she suggested could not be found in the UK at the time but was found somewhere in Europe and eventually I found peace. Having said all that apart from a few episodes on the train I had little trouble. Perhaps the best solution is not to eat very much.

The suburbs of Moscow are somewhat depressing with the remnants of Communism reflected by the concrete high rise hen coops housing Muscovites. My initial companions were two soldiers of about 30 years old who were almost totally bereft of any English. I began to learn that communication is 90% body language and the time passed peacefully. My five words of Russian did not really cut it. Without exception on the trip to Irkusk, which lasted five days, I was shown absolute respect friendliness and generosity. All my fellow travelers were keen to share their food which I subsequently learned is customary on railways but not on planes. My only expressions for days in the light of my Russian and the lack of English from my new friends was "spasibo niet" which I think means "thank you, no." I was embarrassed as I had no food to share thinking I could buy some on the train. I could only trade with vodka but to my surprise this was refused every time. These army officers got off at Novograd and were replaced by a 40-year-old economist, an engineer in his 70s and a store manager in his 30s. The latter used his iPhone to translate to ask me questions. The most uncomfortable one was "do I think Russia is too hostile?" My answer was as diplomatic as I could think of at the time. I suggested the both East and West put their propaganda to the fore and the truth lay somewhere in between. That quelled his curiosity and peace reigned for the rest of their journey apart from heroic snoring from the economist.

The carriage had a side corridor. At one end the inside and outside temperatures were displayed. Outside the temperature was reported from -5C in Moscow falling as we went north to almost -27C. However inside the carriage the temperature was maintained between 20C and 24C from a coal fire. I had not anticipated this and did not have the favored dress of T-shirt and shorts. Slippers would also have been useful. On this train in the washroom was a mat with open criss-cross slats to avoid getting your feet wet from badly aimed male bladder excretions due to the movement of the train. I also bought a mug from the carriage attendant to drink tea. I never drink tea but in the absence of coffee, when in Rome…. What I would have given for a cup of strong black coffee. My itinerary stated I should be given a hot meal per day. When the meal was delivered I found it came on an airline tray with six small bits of chicken warm gravy more rice and a few carrots and beans. To call this a hot meal was underwhelming. On the third day I had new companions one being a middle-aged lady who accepted two meals from the food deliverer. One of the meals was claimed by a fellow traveler who was an Electronics expert and the other I assumed was hers. I asked her on 3 separate occasions it this was her meal and she appeared to answer in the affirmative. I then went to the attendant and deliverer and asked where my meal was. There was obvious confusion and I'm afraid to say I became a little agitated thinking I was going to be denied what I had paid for. Obviously the lack of language was acute so a translator was found in the next carriage who told me I would have to pay for another meal. Somewhat reluctantly I handed over the equivalent of nine dollars for this skimpy repast. Still the cuisine sat in front of this lady until she started producing food of her own and it transpired the meal was mine after all. Major diplomatic dustup narrowly avoided and my money was returned.

At the heavily industrialized Novosibirsk my new friends wished me luck and disembarked. I spied a small middle aged butter-ball lady on the platform. Knowing my luck she would come into my compartment. That was indeed the case although she had some difficulty because the door was not big enough. She brought with her a large polythene bag of rolls and pastries. However she turned out to be a delight despite the language problems. She even gave me her lunch when she realized I had none and refused payment.

Prior to coming on this trip I thought it would be appropriate to see if I could eventually read War and Peace by Tolstoy which I had struggled with during my student days. Perhaps the ambience of the country may make it alive. No such luck. My best endeavors lasted 4 days after which I got fed up reading about the nuances of so-called high society in Moscow in the 19th century. Subsequently I felt very humbled when I learned my son had read both Anna Karenina and War and Peace which he described as a soap opera. Perhaps I will try another time

The scenery was beginning to get somewhat boring as there were trees trees and more trees often birch and pine. These unserried ranks stood straight with their arms hardly bowed with the weight of snow. Siberia would not be the same without snow. Northern Canada shares the same type of vista. In passing the ghostly areas of stripped pines you almost expect a bear to appear or a group of Russian soldiers marching in knee deep snow and singing to blow off the stale fumes of last nights vodka. The scenery became flat and featureless and was only alleviated by a magnificent bright orange sunrise. I cannot imagine the thoughts, fears and hopes of those Jews being transported to the concentration camps in cattle trucks with communal toilet facilities among other dehumanizing treatments.

In all it took 5 days to get to our initial destination of Irkusk the capital of Siberia. The whole line was electrified so there was no reassuring classic interposing click and the ride was very smooth. There was no shower on the train so I solved that problem by not washing for the 5 days. I did not smell any worse than anyone else and no-one complained, mind you no-one could speak English which might have been the explanation. Sometimes ignorance or deafness have their compensations. Or it helps if your sense of smell is poor as is mine. No smelly feet either.

On the 4th day I was getting my 5th cup of tea for the day when I heard voice behind me"Are you British?" My initial shock on hearing a British voice was like music to my ears. When I explained I was Canadian and British and asked how he knew, he replied.

"You are the only one in the carriage wearing a shirt, tucked in and a pen in your shirt pocket. You must be an academic "This was my fellow traveler who I was supposed to meet in Irkusk but he got on the train before that. He turned out to be a Northern Irish 26-year-old labourer on his parents' farm where he raised horses. He had visited 46 countries in his short life and his passport paid testament to that. I suspect he was funded by his mother. We chatted or rather he chatted a lot and I heard his life story within hours. Unfortunately this detracted from the experience of exposure to Russians. Five days is a long time on the train especially as trying to move into another carriage was somewhat dangerous because the linking space was covered with ice. My thoughts were to exercise as much patience as I could because there was nothing to do about the situation. We bypassed several abandoned warehouses with rather depressing small villages characterized by smoking chimneys and small lots. There were occasional cattle and stray dogs but very little else showing signs of life. Perhaps summer would see more animation.

We pulled into Irkusk about 10 o'clock in the evening and again we were immediately met by the tour guide holding a placard with both my name and my traveling companion's name, so that was very easy. Transport was immediately available and we were taken to our small hotel in the center of town. At last a shower. What a wonderful feeling. We went out for a meal and found the portions were about half the size of a North American equivalent. However they were not too expensive. A sleep in a normal bed was restorative and the next morning I realized I would have to get some moon boots to avoid getting my trainers soaking again in the foot deep snow. At that stage I ventured out in the temperature of -17C. At least the locals had the decency to look cold despite wearing several layers and furred hats or hoodies. My search was in vain but when the tour guide arrived she took me to a shoe store where I bought fur-lined boots which turned out ideal. To combat the cold I wore a fur-lined jacket and over-the-top a well-padded anorak. A toque

(Canadian woolly hat) kept my head warm but the leather gloves I thought would be adequate were pitifully not. I should have taken ski gloves. Our first stop on the tour was to visit a memorial to the 20 million Russians who died in the Second World War. It was quite moving. Then we crossed a small bridge to come across the Angara River where it was confluent with the Irkut River and walked along beside the river. We came across a statue commemorating the struggle of women.

Irkusk is the capital of Siberia with a population of almost 600,000. Its main industry is aircraft manufacture. It has a renowned medical school and a university and religious establishments which during the communist era were desecrated and used for other needs. These have now been reestablished. One of the heroes of the white Russians in the 1917 revolution was Alexander Kolchak. He is an interesting character in that he led against the red Russians. He also fell in love with his best friend's wife who joined him and lived together until he was executed after the revolution. In the past most of the houses were wooden and as such were susceptible to fire. The belfry tolled out the message of danger to allow the inhabitants to escape. The belfry still stands. We then went on to see another statute which was Alexander III who was the founder of the trans-Siberian Railway. He was also the father of the last Czar, Nicolas the second, who was shot along with his family after the 1917 revolution. On the statue of Alexander at his feet is a two headed eagle representing head of the state and head of the church. We also visited several churches of Russian Orthodox and Greek Orthodox religions which were architecturally exquisite and inside gold laden. The next day we left to go to Lake Baikal which is the oldest deepest and largest freshwater lake in the world. My friends from Thunder Bay in Ontario claim Lake Superior is the largest but only in surface area. Lake Baikal is 1637 meters deep. On the way we stopped at the village of Talsty. This museum is a recreation of how ancient man lived during the summers in tepee like Birch bark clad dwellings with larders elevated to avoid bears and other animals raiding the food. We also saw how they sliced logs lengthwise, dug them out like a canoe and placed corpses inside then covered them up with the rest of the log and placed them on elevated platforms to avoid animals disturbing them. We also saw how more recently they had a milling system for grain. Irkusk was founded in 1661 and in this village a fort was built in 1667. They also had a small school importing teachers from larger centers with a very handsome salary to work and live in Siberia. We also saw a yurt. We were told these houses are semipermanent made of wood for seminomadic Russians as opposed to the Mongolian totally nomadic houses called gers. We then visited a fascinating museum about Lake Baikal. The visit included a simulated dive to the bottom of the lake and a full explanation of the formation and geology as well as the flora and fauna of the area. It would appear the surroundings have an average of two earthquakes per day albeit minor and small volcanoes and oil leaks deep in the water which are mopped by microorganisms and crustaceans. The most commercial fish is called omul and a personal taste confirmed its delicacy. The lake is drained by the Angara River which means open mouth. We then bought some food for the next journey to Mongolia.

The Mongolian Empire hit its heyday in the 13th and 14th century. It was the largest contiguous land empire in history and spread from central Europe to the Sea of Japan, Siberia India Indochina Iran and Levant and Arabia. Genghis Kahn united various Mongolian tribes and was the ruler of all Mongols in 1206. Since that time Mongolia has shrunk and present-day Mongolia is part of Outer Mongolia: Inner Mongolia lies within China. The attendants on the Mongolia bound train were noticeably more Oriental. One of the problems on all the trains was that the toilets were locked at least 10 minutes before any city or lengthy stop. Of course no one told you when this would happen and it caused quite a bit of distress when you were caught out. I think the only English words the attendant knew were "10 minutes." The water supply was a tiny pipe with a handle which turned on a narrow stream of water descending onto the floor. The trick was to catch it en route. When we left Russia the military and others went through our luggage and compartments mainly to find any illegal passengers. Because we had to change trains the shunting at the border went on for several hours and then the Russian personnel took our Passports for an interminable time and eventually returned them with the appropriate stamp to say that we had left Russia and the visa was in order. We then approached the Mongolian border with a rerun of searching the luggage and compartments and entailed a wait for two hours. On this occasion passports were also taken and a dog was used to sniff out drugs. Then we had another four hour wait for a Mongolian engine. We progressed to Ulan Bator where we were grateful to attend to our bodily functions as the train toilets were locked again. When we vacated our compartment it was locked by the attendant. On arrival our new tour guide welcomed us to the coldest capital of the world.

It has a population of 1.37 million. He told us that Genghis Kahn had 4 official wives, an unknown number concubines, but there were many, and it is estimated he has 40 million descendants today. Russia and Mongolia helped to rid China of the Japanese in World War II. Mongolia is one and a half million square kilometers in size which is 3 times the size of France. There is a general shortage of water making agriculture a challenge in certain areas. The Gobhi desert is suited to the two humped camels which can survive without water for up to 45 days.

We were then taken to our night's accommodation which was a ger. This is a round well insulated canvas tent of substantial proportions with many modern-day appliances including televisions used by the nomadic tribes. It is heated by a central wood and coal burning stove and is warm unless the stove goes out. This was our experience and we had to start the fire on several occasions during the night. We visited a family in a functioning ger. They apparently move four times a year searching for new pastures for their 30 animals which included horses, cattle dogs and hens. The mother proudly told us she has family of eight, obviously created before they got their television set. We visited a remote Buddhist temple where the solitary monk admitted to killing 35 of his relatives as he did not inherit what he thought was his right. When he came to his senses he begged for forgiveness and his atonement was to become a monk. He also turned wheels for us to help with good deeds. We were introduced to the 'ankle bone game' whereby the vertebrae of sheep are thrown to get a score depending which surface showed up with the first past the post winning.

On our return to Ulan Bator we visited various Buddhist temples which were very interesting. Then we noticed a crowd gathering in the central area of the town. We wondered if they had arranged to meet us but in fact it was the visit of the Dalai Lama. He addressed the thousand or so crowd in the square briefly as the temperature was the coldest day for 20 years at -30C. He was wearing only a sparse robe. He promised a fuller speech indoors the next day. The city tour included a visit to the natural history Museum, Parliament Square and the outside of the Houses of Parliament. We were impressed at the architecture of the nearby financial district with high rise glass buildings.

Overall I was not enthralled with Mongolia but my 26 year old traveling companion was which may reflect the age difference.

Onward and upward to China. As we went south through Mongolia the landscape became even more flat and featureless and by the time we reached the Gobi desert the desolation was rampant and forbidding. All of a sudden we spotted sporadic herds of small horses pawing through the snow at the ground in an effort to find something to graze on. On this train a new attendant was not very helpful. I tried to draw his attention to the lack of toilet paper but he just looked at me as if I had 2 heads. Unfortunately my gut problem was recurring and I was getting desperate. I suddenly remembered I had inadvertently packed some tissues which I tore up as necessary and thankfully just made it. However hot water was completely absent. There was evidence of the industry which will make Mongolia extremely rich i.e. mining. Apparently there are vast accumulations of every mineral, apart from diamonds, which have been recently found in Mongolia. The scenery was unrelentingly boring. The lack of stimulation led to wandering innermost thoughts which were similar to meditation. I suppose this goes hand in hand with the Buddhist religion. When we reached the Border again we were searched by the quasi military with the same deal of surrendering passports and waiting. Because the Chinese rail gauge is different from the previous gauge our carriage was lifted off the chassis and put on a new chassis. Quite strange being suspended in air during the process. This exercise took 6 hours at the dead of night. It would have been a lot easier just to change trains.

At daylight we could see the pollution of China's critics with vapors steaming out of vast chimneys and multiple factories. The countryside eventually began to perk up a bit with undulating landscapes and even as we approached Beijing there were almost mountains.

Beijin is a huge city almost fully Westernised and a bit of a disappointment. The architectural styles vary from traditional to box like Stalin-esque blocks of concrete to modern. It is the third most populated city in the world and is subject to smog pollution from nearby industry. It underwent great expansion beginning in the early 80's and now has 6 ring roads. The predominant language spoken is a dialect of Mandarin. Translation of Bejing is northern capital. It contains several UNESCO sites including the Forbidden City and the Temple of Heaven which were built between 1406 and1420. The others include the Summer Palace, the Ming tombs, the Great Wall, the Grand Canal and Zhoukoudian. On 28 October 1420 it was named as the capital of the Ming dynasty.

By now I was the only person on the tour along with a guide so we initially set off for the Great Wall but stopped for a very important visit to the jade factory. This stone is the national emblem for China and the exterior of the factory was very unprepossessing. An in-house guide briefly showed me how the jade was prepared and I was ushered into a huge warehouse full of jade jewelry offered at discount prices. At least that's what I was told. Just the typical tourist thing.

Next up was the Great Wall which is about an hour from the city along a well-made highway. Again the tourist thing: the Great Wall was a fantastic architectural feature crossing mountains and valleys. It has been said that it is the only structure on earth visible from space. There is a lot of controversy about that. The day was absolutely freezing again one of the coldest days of the year with a high wind. The tour guide paid for our admission and as the place was heaving with tourists all slipping on the ice covering I felt it wise to cut the visit to a minimum. I took the appropriate photograph and left. This seem to be much to the tour guide's chagrin but seemed to me to be the better part of valour as I certainly did not want to slip and break a bone so far away from home. We then entered a nearby coffee house to warm up. To say the store sellers were pushy as they showed me round the antique shop attached would be a gross understatement.

After lunch we visited the Ming tombs where 13 of the 16 emperors from that dynasty are buried. By this stage in the trip I was beginning to become fazed by all this information overload so my attention wandered somewhat and I did not retain all the knowledge coming from my guide who was reciting her well-rehearsed speech. However the next visit was to the Summer Palace. This was stimulating with the architecture of the dynasty. I could easily picture those days of emperors and acolytes relaxing in the multicolored buildings. It is a vast ensemble of lakes gardens and palaces. It is 2.9 square kilometers of which three quarters are water. The main features are the Kunming Lake and the Longevity Hill. It was burnt down during the 2nd opium war by an Anglo-French force but since has been rebuilt.

Next day the first visit was to Tiananmen Square. This is one of the largest squares in the world. It comprises 109 acres and it means Gate of Heavenly Peace. Within the square are the Monument to the Peoples Heroes, the Great Hall of the People, the National

Museum of China and the Mausoleum of Mao Zedung. The square is notorious in the Western World for the 1989 massacre. I did not touch on that subject at all with the guide as I saw no benefit in bringing up that controversial subject.

Across the road is the gate to the Forbidden City or the winter palace. Festooned above the gate on the red wall is a huge picture of Chairman Mao Zedung. He declared the People's Republic of China on October 1st 1949. I thought the place was exceptionally busy but the guide told me it was quiet compared with a holiday. They have 14.6 million visitors every year. It was built in 1406 to 1420 and included the Ming and Qing dynasties from 1420 to 1912. It has 980 buildings and covers more than 180 acres. The whole area is arranged with a succession of palaces each coming after a square. The outer or front court was used from ceremonials and the inner or back court for the emperor and family. In the outer court are the Gate of Supreme harmony and the Hall of Supreme Harmony, the Hall of Central Harmony and the hall of Preserving Harmony. The inner court houses the Palace of Heavenly Purity, the Palace of Heavenly Union and the Palace of Earthly Tranquility. The emperor annually prays for a good harvest in the Temple of Heaven. The Ming dynasty were incredibly superstitious and made the roof of the Temple of Heaven blue to represent the sky, and the walls green to represent the earth and yellow the symbol of power. Nine was a sacred number and the steps to the Temple of heaven are arranged in 3 sets of nine. On the way through all these sacred buildings there is a round slightly elevated stone which is said to be the direct communication to heaven. I stood on it as suggested but as yet am waiting for a reply. I hope it was not the direct highway.

The last building before leaving the complex was specially built for the emperor to assess and admit his concubines through the back door. It seems this was quite accepted practice in those days. After all this sightseeing we went to a 'tea tasting'. I do not like tea at the best of times and they did not like that I refused to buy any at their exorbitant prices. It is a different culture but I was not going to be pushed into something I did not want. The guide asked me what I did before retiring. I replied" I used to cut throats" in an off-hand manner. Her face instantly changed from an ever present smile to one of abject horror. "Yyyou used to cut throats" she quailed taking a backward step, wondering what sort of serial killer she was dealing with.

"Yes, but I do not do that anymore, you see I was a head and neck surgeon."

The relief was palpable.

On that high note we parted company and I returned to my hotel to put my feet up before the long flight back home. So I achieved two ticks for the wish list; the Trans-Siberian Railway and going round the world. But I was incredibly happy to be home.

footnote

For anyone wanting to go on this trip I learned the following would be helpful;

- A T shirt and shorts and slippers for the train.
- A penknife for cutting and spreading food
- toilet paper
- soap
- a flashlight or torch
- some form of self-entertainment.

I think it is noteworthy to say I never felt uncomfortable at any time despite the reports of mugging and violence which stimulated many people to say I was brave going alone. If I had a companion we would have spoken to each other and not enjoyed encountering the locals.

I would also thank my wife very much for encouraging me to do the trip before I was too old and putting up with my absence.

AROUND THE WORLD IN 113 DAYS.

'LIFE is a journey, make the most of it'. Unknown. Why do it? We looked forward to retirement but with no specific plan other than that we will not fade away. On the day after his retirement General Norman Schwarzkopf in charge of American soldiers in the Gulf War is quoted as saying "Yesterday I commanded 100,000 troops, today I can't even command my dog." There are many exotic places in the world still to be discovered and this journey fulfilled a lot of those untold stories. We were left a quote almost every day relating to our journey and I'll include some of the more pithy ones.

'To me, travel is more VALUABLE than any stupid piece of bling money can buy'. Raquel Cepeda.

The trip started in Fort Lauderdale. Thankfully my wife had the foresight to allow a day in town before the cruise started. Because we left a day early we managed to avoid one of the most debilitating storms of the year which closed down New Jersey. Fort Lauderdale is well, Fort Lauderdale, quintessentially American, wide boulevards with large cars sprinting and lurching between traffic lights only be held up in another jam. It is the epicentre of ocean cruising closely rivalled by Miami. The city's oceanfront is festooned with high-rise concrete blocks some as high as 30 stories or more. As a lifelong confirmed acrophobic (fear of heights) I could not imagine sitting out on the balcony at the top of these buildings looking down 100 feet or more. By the way vertigo is a term which is derived from the Latin vertiginosus which means to turn, hence it should be reserved for true rotatory dizziness. The port housing the behemoth cruise ships is slightly away from the busy centre of town. I find Florida confusing; on the one hand it is open sunny and somewhat welcoming but on the other hand sterile lacking charm and character.

Embarking on our ship Amsterdam was a tedious event with lines and lines of passengers but the receiving staff processed them relatively quickly. "Do you have your yellow fever card?" Asked the receptionist.

"Yes but we were advised at our age not to have the injection as it has more side effects than the disease" we answered. As we looked around we saw aging characterful faces with a variety of clothing reflecting previous cruises. We think of ourselves as a lot younger than the majority of the passengers until we pass by a mirror. The gangway was lined by glass; I hate this architectural phenomenon as I get systemic weakness and tachycardia (increase in heart rate) when exposed particularly when travelling through airports, Toronto airport being a particularly bad culprit. I don't understand what the fascination with glass is and wish the offending architects could suffer as I do. On board our cabin is deck 2 with a window nicely above the water level but not high like the upper decks with the accompanying balconies to produce high-rise symptoms. The only initial requirement is the lifeboat drill and as normal there is always at least one person who does not understand the clear instructions to assemble at our designated station, but after some consternation she was found at the wrong station. I just hope we never have the situation of having to board the lifeboats in real life. The multiplicity of wheelchairs and motorized scooters as well as walking aids would make the evacuation a nightmare. On the other hand, as was pointed out, the cruise is a fantastic facility for those elderly and infirm who are living in their poorly functioning bodies with perfectly functioning brains. I understood that 75% of the passengers were over the age of 75 years.

Our luggage arrived as promised from our home in Canada but the four cases were impossibly large to store in our cabin. I said to our cabin steward "Robbie, our luggage is far too big for our cabin." "Don't worry I'll take care of it, you can go for your lunch," was his reply. To be fair when we came back to the cabin there was no sign of the luggage and only later did we find our cases hidden under the bed. "I suppose he's done this once or twice before but I find it amazing" I said to my wife. So we only needed hand luggage for the trip from Nova Scotia to Florida.

'I TRAVEL not to cross countries off a list, but to ignite PASSIONATE AFFAIRS with destinations'.

The Cultureur.

After nightfall with minimal fuss the cruise left the dock unnoticed by the chattering diners making new acquaintances and renewing old. It was remarkable to see how often these professional cruisers met up with the reminiscences of previous adventures. As I write this we are passing the northern shores of Cuba soon to dock at Grand Cayman. Our cabin, our home for the next almost 4 months is quite adequate with a queen size bed and cleverly planned storage space for the amount of clothing needed for the voyage. A window gave us the reassuring view of the sea. A television, small desk and sofa completed the cabin as well as an en suite. Just think, no more wondering about what to cook or cleaning or finding entertainment for almost 4 months. Perhaps not a lifestyle but for a short time as a self-retirement prize nothing can beat it. Others make cruising a permanent lifestyle with up to 35 around the world voyages, but with a Presbyterian upbringing we find that difficult.

'You lose sight of things... And when you travel everything balances out'. Daranna Gidel.

That night's entertainment was a very creditable performance in tribute to the pop group ABBA. The audience for this was just about right demographically and my wife and others were up dancing away to the music bringing back memories of yesteryear. "It doesn't matter what you do just do your own thing because you will never see the other passengers again" announced the leader of the band.. The drummer offered to sing a ballad he had made up to the tune of 'let it be' lyrics of which were 'days at sea, days at sea' in continuum reflecting the days at sea.

After two days at sea we arrived at Grand Cayman in conjunction with two other anonymous cruise liners and a downpour. Due to the limitations of docking all the ships were anchored offshore and the participating passengers were transported by tenders to shore. These boats double as lifeboats when necessary. We had previously visited Grand Cayman on a cruise but were somewhat disappointed with the banality of the local architecture and points of interest so opted to swim with the manta rays. They are very friendly and loved to brush by human forms giving both fish and man a thrill. The present weather precluded that. Most other tours involved scuba diving or some other sea sport. On this short trip we decided to continue with our book reading, sudoku and crossword puzzle solving. As it happened we discovered the memory card from our camera had disappeared and the rain stopped so we got on a tender and went ashore to Georgetown. Thankfully a memory card was bought to record our journey. . We had visited the island before and found it dowdy. Today it was even worse. I don't know which is worse Nassau or Georgetown. They redefined the words cheap and tacky and full of tourist 'tat'. Hamilton in Bermuda has gone downhill but not as much compared with these islands.. .The islands are named after a type of shark. I did not see any but there were many two-legged ones giving rise to the notoriety of a tax haven. Back on board my wife went to a lecture on how to understand Windows whereas I looked for the chess companion who had beaten me in three minutes the previous day for a fresh challenge. In the meantime my wife was developing a talent for trivia quizzes which were held several times a day.

'If you wish to travel far and fast, travel light. Take off all your entries, jealousies, unforgiveness, selfishness and fears'. Cesare Pavese.

It was interesting seeing our fellow passengers who were not particularly eclectic as almost all were successful retirees because working people could rarely take four months off. Being of Scottish descent I am a bit reticent for idle chitchat but my wife loves to meet people. In my previous job as a doctor I talked all day every day so I was too tired to talk after a heavy office. Indeed one American once told me I was a work in progress. On the other hand everybody has a story and it was occasionally interesting to share. Tonight it was a

Gala night which meant dressing up in tuxedos and cocktail dresses which pleased my wife. I have to admit I required to loosen the waistband of my trousers. We were sat beside two emeritus professors of linguistics. This is where the egos began to shine. They talked incessantly about themselves. Try as we might we switched off. That was one of the problems with the seating arrangements at the formal dinner so we became much more selective about our dinner partners. The North Americans tend to exchange Christian names only and search for some commonality to prolong discussions as well as an earnest "you must come and visit us".

'If you think adventure is dangerous, try routine, it is lethal'. Paulo Coelho.

Another two days at sea and we arrived at Puerto Limon, Costa Rica which means rich coast. It was named by Christopher Columbus because of all of the gold owned by the natives but in fact the gold came from Peru. It is unique in the fact it has no army and depends on the benevolence of surrounding countries if one is ever needed. Its main export is technology followed by bananas and then coffee. We had briefly visited the country on a previous cruise but despite all the advertising for the booming economy and cheap housing on the Pacific seashore we eschewed further investigation.. This cruise was not only interesting but informative. We learned that bananas develop from a rhizome in nine months from the shoot producing a bunch and the next year a different bunch. As our tour we opted for kayaking downriver in the jungle. In the surrounding heavy foliage we saw wildlife including birds as well as a sloth and monkeys. These latter have a tail used as a third hand and only found in North America. The two of us shared a kayak and required to paddle strenuously on our return upriver against the wind and found muscles which had been long forgotten. A refreshment at the end of the tour was in the form of a coconut with the surrounding copra and coconut chopped off at the top and a straw inserted to suck up the liquid inside. I had not seen this before. Overall we enjoyed the trip but it was not particularly stupendous.

'Travel makes one modest. You see what a tiny place you occupy in the world'. Gustave Flaubert.

The next day we entered the Panama Canal. From here on we were breaking new ground for the next several days. The Panama Canal was begun in 1904 after the revolution one year previously. It is a 80 kilometre waterway with a rise and fall of 85 feet and joins various lakes. Each ship moves 53,000,000 gallons of water and with 35 ships a day water is a premium although the rainfall is 200 inches per year. Seventy five thousand workers were involved in making the canal and 25,000 died, mainly from yellow fever and malaria. They combated mosquitoes producing malaria with a mixture of oil and water. The Culebra Cut was the most difficult to construct going through mountains and subject to landslides producing multiple deaths. The locks pump water in and out to move the ships up-and-down. The lock gates are hollow making less strain on the hinges. Movement of the ships is aided by small train engines on the side of the canal pulling the ships forward.

The next stop was Panama City. We had no idea what this was going to be like and envisaged a small insignificant town but to our complete surprise Panama City has not only a long history but is a vibrant skyscraper bustling financial centre. We opted for a tour of the city with a tour guide who unfortunately did not have good English and had difficulty emphasizing important facts giving insignificant ones the same weight. We would have liked to know more about the importance to the world finances and industry. The walking tour was blistering and humid and the traffic as well as jack-hammers made hearing the tour guide almost impossible. Much of the city centre seemed to be under construction or rather reconstruction and the traffic disrupted our tour. At the end of this day we were very tired and dehydrated and needed to jump in the swimming pool on board to refresh.

The next eight days were spent at sea which in fact we both enjoyed thoroughly with lots of things to do. The sea was calm and it was cloudy. Initially on any cruise the temptation to overeat is incredibly tempting so I started doing a daily gym effort. Treadmill and weights were my tools to avoid weight gain and also I attended a bridge class to understand the basics of this challenging game. Lesley went to water colouring painting classes as well as drawing classes and developed great talent. Lesley was also keen on trivia quizzes but my only contribution was to correctly identify the reason for somebody who could not ride his horse somewhere in America, the answer being haemorrhoids. This by the way was also the reason for Napoleon's defeat at Waterloo. The artist in residence teaching us how to draw was excellent and flamboyant reflecting his artistic personality. He taught the basics of shapes so that drawing portraits or other interesting scenes became easy. Unfortunately I cannot draw a straight line so I opted out of the drawing but was fascinated by his talks on the history of art. Microsoft employed someone on board to talk about their products. Unfortunately again I did not have the knowledge or expertise to fully benefit from these talks. My bridge lessons were getting complicated and I did not care for the teacher particularly so again I opted out this but played a simplified game with a pleasant American lady." You don't have to play that complicated game we are being taught, I have played for many decades in a simplified version which is just as enjoyable" she said. Another diversion was to 'name that tune'. Some of Lesley's trivia companions held a cocktail party in their upmarket cabin which was very pleasant meeting some other co-passengers. We crossed the equator for the first time but without any celebration which is a little disappointing but we crossed the equator on four occasions altogether so celebrations were withheld until the last one.

'As you move through this life... You leave MARKS behind, however small. And in return life and travel leaves marks on you'. Anthony Bourdain.

There were interesting characters on board including Lynn a retired nurse who worked in the Congo, Bob and Marsha who owned an IT company, and Keas and Alexander who were nuclear physicists and computer experts. Robert and Bill were a retired gay couple who

Lesley joined doing trivia and were great companions throughout the voyage. These two were almost professional cruisers. They had booked another cruise just after this one. In fact there was one lady who had been on a world cruise 35 times. Apparently she never worked a day in her life. Jackie an over 80-year-old American retired teacher was sharp as a tack and taught me a lot about bridge and in return I taught her Sudoku. Lesley enjoyed the trivia questions but I was somewhat inflamed when the so-called answers were wrong so I decided to forgo that pleasure. I found the majority of the Americans were pleasant and outgoing but was to find later on this was not for all Americans. There was a gala night tonight followed by a masked ball. It sounds very exotic and exciting but in fact there were far too many people for the dance area and when we danced our seats were taken as soon as we turned round. There was no point in arguing so and confrontation usually ends up negative so we decided to return to our cabin and watched a movie.

Another day at sea with bridge and I attended the Microsoft tutorial on how to Skype and make interesting photographs. Another day at sea and the evening entertainment was absolutely dreadful with dancing and singing. Not being an expert in Opera, although I had experience of seeing opera singers as an ear nose and throat surgeon when they attended Edinburgh Festival, even I could tell the singers could not hold a note. I was reliably informed that this was vibrato but this was very poor. However Lesley enjoyed them.

'We travel, some of us forever, to seek other places, other lives, their souls". Anais Nin.

Our next stop was TAIOHAE, NUKU HIVA in French Polynesia. At last land. It was roasting and bright and we awaited tenders to take us on over to our tour. We were greeted on the dock by beautiful traditionally dressed ladies with accompanying Hawaiian style of music. In fact this welcoming became routine at subsequent ports. The surrounding scenery was lovely with mountains rising steeply and covered with trees. We climbed into a 4 x 4 vehicle. The road we took was very high and winding with a precipitous drop. Unfortunately the driver could only speak French so I tried my best with schoolboy French that was not particularly successful. We drove up high and then down into the valley to palm trees and coconut groves. The scenes have proven to be a backdrop for several movies. We were told that the tourism industry was in its infancy which became obvious from the lack of interesting stops. I was very disappointed with the whole trip but again Lesley enjoyed it. This trip was particularly overpriced which detracted from the experience. We were told that Herman Melville the author of Moby Dick and Typee was stimulated to write the latter novel from his experience on the island so he obviously enjoyed his stay.

Thereafter followed a succession of putting the clocks back between 30 minutes and one hour every two or three days.

'Travel is at its most rewarding when it ceases to be about your reaching a destination and becomes indistinguishable from living your life' Paul Theroux.

AROUND THE WORLD IN 113 DAYS 2

'When was the last time you did something for the first TIME'? Live learn evolve.

Another day at sea and then we arrived at Rangiroa. This is a small island still in French Polynesia and unfortunately on the Sunday we arrived most things were closed. So we walked from the beach into the town which is very small. We commented on the sea which was a deep azure blue washing up on the coral beaches. Not a lot there.

'When in doubt, TRAVEL'. Anonymous.

The next stop was Papeete, Tahiti which was fiery and humid. We had high expectations of this visit but unfortunately they were not met. On our tour we visited the house of James Norman Hall who was an adventurer soldier, a highly decorated pursuit pilot, famous author, essayist, poet and beloved father. He authored at least 16 novels and co-authored 12 novels. Several movies have been based on the island including Mutiny on the Bounty three times, The Hurricane twice and others. There are 118 islands in French Polynesia, 70 are inhabited of whom six were noted as the Society Islands founded by Capt. Cook. Overall there was not a lot to see although the vistas were spectacular. Unfortunately Papeete itself is very touristy and cheap and tawdry similar to Port-au-Prince, Haiti and Grand Cayman.

'The world is a book and those who do not travel read only one page'. St. Agustine.

Moorea, our next stop, was a beautiful island and we decided to take a catamaran tour. Overall it was a lovely day. We were late getting to the tender as our watches were running slow. The excuse could be the number of time changes we made on our voyage because going west we encountered multiple losses of 30 minutes to an hour with the time changes. Thankfully the catamaran waited for us at a distant pier. The wind was high and the hulls pushed through the increasing swell and white horses. After about half an hour of thrusting through the oncoming wind we headed starboard to a beautiful bay giving us a respite from the conditions. Our tour guide proceeded to tell us the legend behind the formation of the nearby islands. A God stood on Tahiti and hurled a spear through Moorea's Mountain leaving a hole near the summit which is seen today and took the displaced rock further on to make another island. We then turned and sailed with the wind. The sensation brought back very fond memories of my time in Bermuda with a slap of the waves against the hulls, the sun, the incidental spray, at one the feeling of freedom reminiscent of Jonathan Livingston Seagull by Richard Bach. The soporific undulations reviving basic human reactions in infancy to a mother's nursing. Oh, how I miss those halcyon days with friends, laughter and problems disappearing albeit only briefly forgotten. These sensations were topped by a sharp refreshing snorkel. Lesley found some Maori statues called teki in the water as well as fluorescent fish and I saw a manta ray." That was great, I really loved seeing all these fishes in the warm water. Again just like Bermuda," she said. A refreshing rum punch sealed the tour.

'Explore, dream, discover'. Mark Twain.

Bora Bora is in fact pronounced Pora Pora as there is no B in the Tahitian language. It is a nice group of islands with beautiful views but expensive. On our bus tour there were few places of interest and we were disappointed to see the poor houses with corrugated tin roofs as a result of the recurrent hurricanes which frequent the South Pacific. The sea approach is by a single channel but the port became important following the bombing of Pearl Harbour in World War 2. We were invited to refresh at the Bloody Mary restaurant which has been visited by many celebrities but were shocked at the prices so they did little business with our tour group.

The next day at sea meant an interesting talk of the geology of the South Pacific and the drawing class sketched Michelangelo's David.

Rarotonga, one of the Cook Islands, was difficult to approach with no anchorage and a heavy swell . No walking aids apart from canes were allowed on the tenders which was unfortunate for the disabled so only those who could walk could enjoy the island. It was originally an English colony and got its independence in 1968. Cars drive on the left. Our bus tour showed us some lovely sights but few places of interest. Another sea day followed.

'I need Vitamin SEA'. Anonymous

Next stop was Alofi Niue. Again a small island with a sea swell making the landing difficult. Religion is important so as it was Sunday we were told not to swim near the church. As expected there was very little to see but we took a picture of government house and a law firm suggesting that if all else fails my son and stepson could take their profession there. If truth be told overall our visits to Polynesia did not meet our expectations. We had followed the advertisements for the luxurious lifestyle of the islands but as I had discussed with a previous tourist the South Pacific is a very large place and the travel is not rewarded by actuality. Perhaps there was a certain sameness about the islands in a similar vein to the Caribbean islands.

Unfortunately I overdid the gym and hurt my back resulting in agony requiring heavy analgesia. We both slept well that night and crossed the international dateline which meant Monday, January 29 did not happen. All of a sudden we are in Tuesday and January 30. That is a loss of a day going East to West, going West to East gains a day which would mean two Mondays. Confusing? I stopped being gluttonous only having one course at breakfast and lunch and managed to lose 4 pounds. The captain who regaled us on a daily basis about the meteorological and navigational details warned us we are about to be hit by a gale and to stow everything tight. As it so happened there was some rain and increased swell but not nearly as bad as advertised and we hoped it would stay that way. Unfortunately the next day the rain became heavier and the swells increased. We were told we were caught between two systems between Australia and Rarotonga. The next day the swells became less and without rain. The sun came out and Lesley modelled jewellery at a fashion show on board.

Two more days at sea brought us to Auckland, New Zealand. I had mixed emotions revisiting the city where I sat the inevitable exam and became a fellow of the Australasian College of Surgeons. It was 35 years since I had last been there and obviously there's a lot of new development. Both Australia and New Zealand have very strict laws about importing food so none was allowed from the ship. We docked in Queen Street which is in the heart of the city and really it could be anywhere. There's a lot of construction and high-rises all over. The population of New Zealand has now reached 4.2 million, when I was there it was only 3 million. Auckland itself has 1.4 million. It has been built on 147 volcanoes but no very large ones. There is a huge farmland area in the middle of the town called Cornwall Park, a great lung for the city. We took a private tour through their congested streets almost like driving in London England. There are lots of small areas and villages within the city and the horizon is dominated by the Sky Tower. House prices in the city range up to NZ$1 million or more but they are more reasonable elsewhere. I recall New Zealand used to be a haven for vintage cars or just plain old cars. Now apparently Japan offloads its cars when they reach the age of eight years and sends them to New Zealand with the result now there are lovely rust free automobiles on the roads. New Zealand is now a multicultural society including Polynesians, Americans, Canadians and British. It is interesting that Chinese immigrants cannot buy a house, they have to build a house. I remember the paranoia about the potential Chinese overwhelming immigration to New Zealand. Our tour guide was very proud that New Zealand won the America's Cup in Bermuda last year. Now Dubai wants to host next Cup at the cost of many billions. Now at least half of the crew must be from the country they are representing. Also only single hulls are allowed.

'To travel is to awaken'. Lily Tsay.

Tauranga

This is a huge port servicing most of New Zealand. We took a bus tour to the other side of Rotorua to see the world-renowned steaming thermal pools. I had previously visited Rotorua with nearby thermal pools so cannot understand why we had to travel to the other side of Rotorua. I am very cynical about the tours and wondered what deal had been made. Eventually after some considerable time the bus pulled up on the wrong side of a lake and we had to pay $36 to get in the boat across the lake to the geysers. The hillside display was reasonable but not fantastic. Lesley went right to the top of the hill to take a panoramic picture. We had a quick sandwich, then bus began its return stopping at Wai-o-tapu a much closer thermal pool. For another $30 we could see this one but opted not to although it is said to be much prettier. Further on we stopped to take pictures of bubbling mud. There was not much to see in Rotorua town itself. We returned to the ship in time to miss the emergency drill but Lesley managed her trivia.

'The JOURNEY is the DESTINATION'. Dan Eldon.

A visit to Te Puke, the kiwifruit capital of the world it is claimed, informed us of the different types, green and gold. We also learned that growing avocados is facilitated by grafting the rootstock similar to grape cultivation.

'WANDERLUST. A strong desire for our impulse to wander or TRAVEL and explore the world'. Anonymous

The next port was Napier, North Island which is a lovely seaside town with a delightful esplanade. Its main business is tourism. The grape industry was just beginning at my first visit but this has burgeoned enormously. A large export is pinewood. Overall it was a lovely day with lovely people.

'TRAVEL is FATAL to prejudice bigotry and narrow mindedness'. Mark Twain.

Another day at sea before Dunedin. We were delayed in docking because another cruise ship, twice our size, had docked first and the wind made the manoeuvre tricky. Again there was a high gangway with glass sides but the more I was exposed to heights the marginally easier it became. A bus took us to the centre of the town from the dock in about 20 minutes. I had had high expectations of the city because of its close relation to our birthplace, Edinburgh. Overall I was disappointed and felt from the architecture we could be almost anywhere apart from the municipal building, the Cathedral and the statue of Robert Burns. There was very little to remind us of our home town. The railway station was pleasing to the eye, but the showers on and off made us feel cold. The bright spot was lunch at the Best Café which served up the nicest fish and chips I can remember. Having nearly put the rest of my life in this land I have mixed thoughts about returning. The land is beautiful, picturesque, green and almost idyllic if it were not for the people. Outwardly friendly but there lies an undercurrent of an inferiority complex to the rest of the world. Geographically isolated it is an impossible distance from anywhere. Thirty five years has seen a large step forward to join the planet with high-tech and better cars. Given the bad treatment I was shown here on my previous visit and the intellectual barrenness I doubt it could have been a long-term solution to my career. On the other hand my spell in Scotland had its problems as well.

'We WANDER for distraction, but we TRAVEL for fulfilment'. Hilarie Belloc.

Our next sojourn was to the Fjord National Park on the West Coast of South Island. The iconic fjord is the Milford Sound. There are several sounds nearby but this one is the most spectacular. The sides are unbelievably steep sheer out of the water with snow-capped ridges. An incredible sight. The mountains rise more than 3000 feet perpendicularly. It was named after Milford Haven in the UK. Nearby there are several islands which have been rendered pest free to encourage near extinct birds such as the Takahe bird to flourish.

'Once a year, GO SOMEPLACE you've never been before'. Dalai Lama.

Welcome to Sydney! The crossing of the Tasman Sea was fairly calm and the only thing of note was a previous New Zealand Prime Minister nicknamed Piggy Muldon who is quoted as saying 'every time a New Zealander crosses the Tasman Sea the average IQ of both countries goes up'. The harbour is one of the most beautiful in the world according to Capt. Jonathan Mercer. We approached at dawn with an overcast sky and most of the guests accumulated on the veranda deck. Amazingly rude a lot of these passengers were who commandeered a superior photographic position and refused to let others to take their photographs. Disembarkation was a trial for me with my acrophobia. The exit was from deck three necessitating walking through the glass enclosed walkway down 2 stories then on to an escalator. Queues and lines were inevitable with passports presented by ourselves and then reclaimed by the Holland America personnel. Our tour bus took us to the Sydney Opera House. There is a picturesque tourist type walkway providing excellent views of the iconic Sydney Harbour Bridge which some of our recently acquired 'friends' set off to climb to the top. Crazy. The tour to the opera was compromised because it was the opening night of Carmen and the main theatre was used for a rehearsal and therefore out of bounds for us. What a disappointment to be shown backstage with no opportunity to sample the acoustics of the operatic auditorium. The building's architect was Jorn Utzon whose original concept apparently came to grief on several points, including finance, being rejected by the panel of judges deciding the format in the 1950s. However he was forgiven and eventually finished off the job. The featured lines of the roofs are well recognized across the globe and set in the Sydney Harbour backdrop to complete a magical and majestic command of the area. The tour of the opera house was extremely disappointing, particularly as we were overrun by myriads of Chinese. The bus then drove through the hinterland of the city of 4.2 million population bringing back reminiscences of villages and suburbs of London England. The city seemed stretch interminably up to 50 km we were informed. Some of the suburbs seem to be very expensive, nice but not awe-inspiring. Eventually we arrived at the world-renowned Bondi beach. Despite having seen pictures I was still gob smacked at the extent of the beach and the volume of exposed flesh of the younger generation. There seemed to be no inhibitions in sun tanning; I wonder if they have ever heard of melanoma?

On the land side of the beach are several cafés. Passing by brought back memories of the cacophony of a gannet colony on a sea-based rock. The gaggle was an overwhelming babble, incomprehensible although the players seem to understand each other perfectly well. A delayed but rapidly ingested cheeseburger and a beer drunk in the wrong unlicensed Café sufficed to assuage the pangs of hunger and hypoglycemia stimulated grumpiness. Altogether Sydney came over as okay but the traffic was unbelievable and not a place I would like to return to. As typical of a teaming metropolis downtown is marked by high-rise offices and residences with some genuine classic architecture of the beginnings of the colony. It was noticeable that the street names reflected those of the founding fathers of the city from England. In April 1770 James Cook landed at Botany Bay. Sydney was first founded on 26 January 1788 when 11 ships with 1400 people convicts, soldiers and others landed at the Rocks where they first erected their tents. It has now become an upmarket suburb. We overnighted at Sydney Harbour and the next day ventured back into the city. Great waves of humanity spilled out onto the streets. My wife left me to go shopping so I had the opportunity to study the onslaught. Pretty young and unattached teenage girls daring to bare as much flesh as was decent, young moms pushing their babies in prams and walkers, different tones of skin, many language snippets and all wanting to be seen rather than actually shop. And like any other large city with the pleasant anonymity of not caring about best behaviour. In another pedestrian precinct street performers pedalled their trade – guitar players, conjurers and immobile statues. Men are from Mars and there is no shopping there. By the time we got back to the ship it was too late to do any other tours so we looked forward to cast off heading to our port in Tasmania. The Sydney tour was bad. We didn't get to see the main auditorium of the opera house with acoustics and we have liked to see. The tour in the town was on the bus and the buildings only noticed in passing. My suggestion is if the opera is not fully open to tailor the tour to see more architecture. It never ceases to amaze me how these extremely high-rise offices can be built immediately adjacent to water. Obviously it works but the engineering and geology and architecture are amazing.

'Travel while you are YOUNG and able. Don't worry about the MONEY, just make it work. EXPERIENCE is far more valuable than money will ever be'. Anonymous

Each city we had visited seemed similar except some unique landmarks. Is this the Western influence to normalize everything to be the same?

'Take every CHANCE you get in life, because some things only happen ONCE'. Karen Gibbs.

We were going through the Bass Strait when typically the weather started acting up. At first the seas were only slightly choppy when we arrived in Hobart, Tasmania, under clouds but entered a beautiful harbour. It is very protected and ideal for this purpose. Thankfully the gangway was only from deck one so it was not too anxiety provoking. We decided to do a hop on hop off bus which in theory was a good idea. The city was very pleasant with an excellent pedestrian precinct but otherwise not noteworthy. The next bus was never coming around so we walked back to the ship.

The weather started closing in and a storm force 5 to 6 was planned for Hobart so Capt. decided to give Port Arthur a miss and went to the east of Tasmania in the lee. The seas were a bit rough so the ship was slowed down and headed into the wind in a northwesterly direction towards Kangaroo Island. The storm built up with lots of rain and from deck nine the panoramic view was obscured. Overnight I lost my pencil sharpener overboard into the depths of the Bass Strait! What a disaster, I could not continue my blog with blunt pencils. The Valentine ball was cancelled! I thought it would be nice for Lesley to have a dozen red roses which I ordered. The seas were getting heavier and with one bad lurch the red roses were careered across the cabin as was the glass vase. The seas became so bad it was dangerous to continue at 16 knots so we slowed to 3 knots and in fact hove to ie. Stopped. The boat was still very unstable but we were promised that things would settle next day. I thought our ship Amsterdam was fairly large to easily outride the storm but compared with some other cruisers it was referred to as the blue canoe. However there was no real panic on board and everybody was cleared from the outside decks. The next day the sea had settled a bit and we were informed by the captain the swell had been 26 feet with gale force winds. Apparently this area is very prone to bad weather. We went back up to 16 ½ knots steering to the West despite the increased swell and rain. It was overheard in the restaurant when the captain's wife was asked at her evening meal 'are you expecting your husband to join you for dinner?' 'Hell no, he's on the bridge'. Clocks back again and I was so confused I did it twice. At last calm seas again and the speed increased to make up the time to get to Kangaroo Island.

'I haven't been everywhere but it's on my LIST'. Susan Sontag.

AROUND THE WORLD IN 113 DAYS 3

'To travel is to live'. Hans Christian Andersen.

Kangaroo Island. This was a desolate small dorp so we decided not to go to town because of the bad reports. Despite the name of the island we never saw any kangaroos. There was a cold spreading throughout the ship and I think Lesley may have the beginnings. I have no idea why this port was chosen by previous passengers and I certainly voted against it on this occasion. This is Chinese New Year with lanterns and Chinese paraphernalia in the dining room where there is no need for formal dress as opposed to the waiter service in the other dining room where formal dress was required. I'm looking forward to going to Adelaide tomorrow. The entertainment tonight was awful and I left; Lesley thought it was wonderful.

'TRAVEL in the younger sort, is part of EDUCATION, in the elder, a part of EXPERIENCE". Francis Bacon.

Adelaide was a lovely city with nice wide roads and well laid out. Our tour took us to Cleland Park where we saw lots of different animals, and hand fed kangaroos. The quiche for lunch was absolutely fabulous and the views from Mount Lofty over the city were superb. The population is 1.2 million. The stores and malls were much the same as anywhere else with Target and Woolworth's. The port where we docked is neglected with vacant decrepit factories. Apparently two passengers were removed in handcuffs from the ship probably due to drugs and their state room was taken apart particularly in the ceiling. On the dock there were hundreds of new cars because the car industry has been withdrawn from Australia and all cars are imported.

'To travel is to live'. Hans Christian Andersen.

Albany was the last place in Australia for troops going to World War I. It is a one horse town. At last the gangway was flat and short. Why it that physically disabled people is are given priority while I have acrophobia and no one pays any attention to that? The bay we entered was very nice and possibly second only to Sydney. And the shore side Café had free Internet. The town population appeared to double when the ship docked. I don't understand why the ship goes to these crummy places when over 800 voyagers are repeating and want to go to other ports. On the other hand some passengers liked small places. I personally like historic buildings and architecture. My suggestion is a different route for 2020 round the world voyage but I'm not sure if I really want to go on another.

'No more than ever do I realize that I will never be content with a sedentary life, that I will always be haunted by thoughts of a sundrenched elsewhere'. Isabelle Eberhardt.

'Another day at sea and we arrived at Fremantle. We disembarked from deck three but the gangway was short and covered so not so anxiety provoking or perhaps I am becoming desensitized. Fremantle is a port, the town is small and pleasant with some old buildings. Some of the warehouses have been converted and there are several new buildings. One of note is the roundhouse which was originally a prison. We took a train to the city of Perth. On our tour there we visited several millionaire residences and went on to Kings Park which was beautiful overlooking the Swan River. The Perth skyline is very impressive and there are several motorways connecting the city. It has beautiful new architecture with glass buildings and sensibly is not overcrowded. The bus service is free in Fremantle and Perth and although they are 12 miles apart the buildings are almost continuous. We stopped off at the beautiful Cottisloe beach on the way home. Perth has a population of 1.4 7 million and the beaches were quite clean. Lesley felt that if she was 20 she would move there. "It's got everything". Again hundreds of cars were lined up on the wharf being imported. So that was the last of Australia and the next part of the voyage I hoped it would be a lot more interesting and different from Western society.

'Nothing behind me, everything ahead of me, as is ever so on the road'. Jack Kerouic.

Entertainment that night were the so-called divas singing again to screeching levels. I suppose 75% of the audience had a high tone sensorineural hearing loss and could not hear the high notes. Hearing aids proliferated. In fact there are very few places on board free of unnecessary so-called recorded music and even in the library people talk loudly at each other. In any event I lasted about five seconds for the entertainment. Even Celine Dion's recording was screaming, like bagpipes welcoming tourists; awful. I have tinnitus so probably suffer more than most.

My emotions and feelings for the first part of this around the world voyage were really unremarkable in that it seemed to be same old same old. I hope the next part will alleviate that ennui.

There were three sea days to Bali. My only claim to fame on the whole voyage was doing a sport in which I have zero interest and zero talent, golf. I happened across a lot of men standing in line down a staircase and then I realised Lesley was officiating at the men's putting. I stood in line and when my turn came the course was to putt from several steps up the staircase down to the deck where the hole was. I putted in a desultory fashion and the ball trickled towards the hole and just at the moment critique the ship lurched and my ball fell in the hole! A hole in one! I thought I was wonderful alas Lesley did not agree. In any event I resigned at the top of my game and resisted attempts to reproduce the miracle. I also turned down the offer to buy everyone on board a drink as I am told is the custom after a hole in one. Drinks for 1600 people would wipe out my budget and more!

The Captain informed us we would be passing through pirate territory so we had to make some preparations. So we arrived at Bali the port being Benoa with a flat gangway, hurrah! We went on a privately organized tour but were delayed so missed the dancing we were supposed to see. We saw some weaving of cloths but as usual on the tourist trip it was a rip off. The thing that comes to mind is the struggle with the horrendous traffic overwhelming the road system with the incessant buzzing of motor bikes and scooters which apparently outnumber the actual population. Indonesia is a country with 70,000 islands but only 7000 are populated. The population is said to be 270 million and is said to be the third most populated nation. We were warned not use a credit card as the likelihood of this being copied was high. We then went to Sangeh monkey forest which contained interesting architecture with many temples, a distinctive green mould on rocks and hundreds of macaque monkeys. These are small, long tailed and omnivorous. Their main foods are sweet potato, banana, papaya leaf, corn, cucumber and coconut. One tried to pick my breast pocket, another sat on my hat on top of my head. I hoped they did not carry rabies, so far so good. We then had a long trip to Kintamini a beautiful place overlooking the slopes of Mt Batur where we had lunch. Perhaps this is not the ideal place for me because there was a huge drop right next to where we were supposed to eat and the buffet meal consisted of noodles which I don't eat. So I didn't and was not in a good mood particularly as there was no air conditioning in our minibus. Although we saved more than $200 by not going on the official ships tour it really was not worth it. We had been advised by a fellow passenger who thought she knew it all to go on the private tour but given the rest of the expenses this was not a good idea. Our second day in Bali we visited a temple, Daya Tarik Wisata Tanah Lot, renowned we were told for the wonderful beach. We envisaged stretches of white pleasant sand but were more than a little disappointed to find minimal amounts of our expectations and mainly rocks. This was a total waste of time. The only excitement was a large branch of a palm tree fell down 2 feet away from me, a narrow escape. We had to pass a lot of vendors on the way out and were almost physically attacked to buy cheap T-shirts and other rubbish. The next stop after a one and a half hour drive was to see some rice fields and a nice restaurant for lunch. However given the previous experience we took sandwiches fruit and water from the ship as nobody told us not to. After lunch the next stop was another temple, the Royal Temple,Taman Ayun built in 1634 AD in the reign of King of Mengui to worship the royal ancestors and evoke prosperity for the people of the kingdom. The entrance fee only allowed us to walk around and not go inside. This was another unnecessarily long trip. The business of tourism was overwhelming and aggressive with physical contact from the vendors to persuade a transaction. I vowed to myself not to repeat the Bali experience.

'A good traveller has no fixed plans, and is not intent on arriving'. Lao Tzu.

AROUND THE WORLD IN 113 DAYS 4

'There is still SO MUCH to see'. Anonymous.

The next three days were sea days so we had a practice run to deal with any possible pirates. The crew were stationed outside on the decks dressed in full body armour including facemasks and helmets. Passengers were to stand in the corridors away from any portholes or Windows and the crew practiced antipirate manoeuvres. The captain issued a letter as follows:

During our transit of the Indian Ocean, towards Victoria, Seychelles we will enter the Indian Ocean high risk area. There has been a significant decrease in incidents in the past few years, nevertheless, it would be inconsiderate not to take precautions.

They include:

1. Amsterdam will be reporting regularly to UKMTO in Dubai. UKMTO is the United Kingdom Maritime Trade Organization who coordinates all of the coalition warships in the area assigned to antipiracy operations. We are being tracked during our transit and although we may not see them, warships are not far away.

2. A close radar watch will be kept on the bridge.

3. We have extra security guards and they will be rotating a 24-hour antipiracy watch.

4. We have four LRADs (long-range acoustic devices) rigged, manned and ready for immediate use. These are designed to paralyse any attackers with focused loud noises.

5. We will also have charge of water hoses ready for use on both sides of the lower promenade deck.

6. We are making high-speed, always a good deterrent.

In the unlikely event of an attempted boarding or even if we are suspicious of a vessel you will hear one long ring of the ships alarm followed by an announcement; testing, testing, testing from the captain, staff captain or the officer on watch on the bridge. Upon hearing the announcement you are asked to move out of your staterooms and stay in corridors or an interior space, please move from the outside decks. Stay away from windows and doors; please sit down, as any manoeuvres attempted by myself may result in heeling of the ship as we will be moving at high speed, we are capable of 25 knots.

'We need the possibility of escape just as surely as we need hope'. Edward Abbey.

We crossed the equator last night at 9 PM but thankfully no pirates. I had difficulty sleeping so I went out on the deck two stern to find one of the security guards complete with computer, telescope and other paraphernalia to identify any potential attackers. The Capt. had speeded up to 19 knots through the danger area. After that we settled down to 14 knots

The entertainment in the evening was poor with singers off key and flat and amateurish with the usual poor vibrato. There was also a so-called mentalist who claimed to see inside minds and set up with members of the audience some tricks. He said he was a professional poker player and magician and had been a mentalist for one year. He claimed to cure joint pains with hypnosis and superficially it sounded good but I suspect most of it was psychosomatic or a fake. He claimed to cure a passenger with a post radiation neck lacking in saliva but in the end the patient was fed up with the prolonged treatment and just said he was cured to end the session.

'ALL JOURNEYS have secret destinations of which the traveller is UNAWARE' Unknown.

Puerto Princesa. Philippines. The last visit of the Amsterdam in 2013 heralded the pilot coming on board from a dugout canoe! It was steaming and humid and thankfully a shuttle bus took us to a shopping mall. This was depressingly similar to North American malls. The traffic was dense with both cars motorcycle taxis and people. The city was founded on January 1, 1970. Some passengers went to the Subterranean River national Park to see one of the world's longest underground rivers necessitating part of the trip in Outrigger canoes. There were unique rock formations and cathedral like chambers. When we docked for Manila we found four cruise ships in at once and again encountered horrendous traffic. It was 34°C and wilting. We went to Tagaytay to see the smallest volcano in the world, the Taal volcano which is a volcano surrounded by a lake within a volcano. We had a brief tour of Manila which is full of high-rise buildings and depressingly Americanized. It has been in turn invaded by Spanish British and Japanese as well as Americans. They have each left a rich legacy. The road signs are in English and one of the legacies of America are the presence of jeepneys. These are large taxis or small buses with very colourful decorations being one of the main sources of transport. There are few regular buses and no underground system. The city seemed to be mainly concrete with multiple high flyovers. We had a police escort for our buses as otherwise we could not move because of the traffic density. In Manila we visited the old city of Intramuros (between the walls). Traditionally wealthy people lived in the area. Although Imelda Marcos, of a thousand pairs of shoes fame, had a poor reputation internationally she did a lot for the Filipinos culture and new buildings. At present there is a major clampdown on drug pushers and dealers. In the hinterland high-rise buildings proliferated in the process of construction. They are trying to make a "city of dreams" with multiple casinos which abound not only in Manila but also throughout the island. The gangway was from deck one and I loved it. Much of new Manila is on reclaimed land. I wanted to see Intramuros more closely so we hired a taxi. This taxi consisted of a motorbike with a side attachment for Lesley which was just at exhaust level and she inhaled copious amounts of carbon monoxide. I was on the pillion with my feet on the motor bikes exhaust which melted my sneakers. The traffic was awful and the young driver did not know his way around and we got lost. Overall it was very frightening and I was hanging on for grim death. For me this ranked among the worst lifetime experiences. I could not think of any worse at the time. We were very pleased to finish the tour. There was not a lot to see anyway.

'TRAVELLING. It leaves you SPEECHLESS, then turns you into a STORYTELLER'. Ibn Battuta.

AROUND THE WORLD IN 113 DAYS 5

'Travel is... Getting to know yourself by facing new EXPERIENCES'. Sofie Cowenbergh, Wonderful Wanderings.

'Not I, not anyone else, can travel that road for you, you must travel it for YOURSELF'.

Walt Whitman.

The next port of call was Hong Kong. This is a very busy harbour with a one-way system for boats entering and leaving. The ex-colony has a population of 7.5 million over 1100 km². It consists of the Kowloon Peninsula, New Territories and Hong Kong Island. It has a considerable amount of reclaimed land with multiple high-rise buildings. We were told the tallest is 118 stories and sways 3 metres in a typhoon. It is traffic bound despite the hundred percent tax on cars. We were delayed at immigration for about an hour. The gangway was high with several arms again with glass sides but I was not quite so anxious. The first stop on the tour was a flower market which was enormous and understandably all the flowers were imported from Indochina and Vietnam. There is no room in Hong Kong to grow them. Around the corner was a bird market where several hundred birds were in cages all contributing to the general ambient noise. I somehow don't think this would be tolerated in the UK or North America. This was followed by a visit to a floating restaurant in Aberdeen harbour. It is named after George Aberdeen who at the time of founding was the UK Prime Minister. The lunch was typically Chinese with all carbohydrates. After that came the Stanley market with all sorts of merchandise and was ideal to hone my haggling skills. Next stop was the Temple Street market under canvas; the sole commodity on sale was Jade which the Chinese revere. Yet another market was the Jewel Factory Limited. That is one of the downsides of being a tourist being hawked around these magnets. One has to be fairly hard headed to say thank you but no. I experienced this in a previous visit to Beijing. The tour continued to

Victoria Peak where unbelievable high-rise residences and expensive houses are juxtaposed to government funded apartments. The descent was suggested in a funicular cable car which Lesley took but I stayed on the bus. Lesley loved the day with all the bustle but I was not quite so enamoured. There is a big United Kingdom influence after independence in 1997 without full integration with China. It will be several decades before that can be achieved. Driving is on the left and there were double deck buses as in the UK. The traffic was not as bad as Bali or Manila. There are 8 golf courses on the island each with a joining fee of $3 million Canadian. A small apartment (180 ft.^{2}) was very expensive and with a minimal wage of six dollars per hour it seems impossible to be afforded. A lot of these houses are built on very steep hills. I had been offered after qualification to go to either Hong Kong or South Africa and I'm pleased I chose the latter. We stayed another day and walked to the Ocean terminal which is very pleasant with some interesting architecture and upmarket stores. There was a short distance to the subway to the main shopping district. There was nothing to buy there for us. The road signs were in both Cantonese and English. The whole city reminded me of George Orwell's 1984 with everything too well-organized and routine. The crowds and traffic in the streets were reminiscent of Dante's version of Hell with everyone dashing about their business and nobody caring about anyone else. Perhaps this is a reflection of a big city. Youths staring into handheld machines and even talking to them oblivious of traffic dangers, ear plugs dangling. Like rats living in coops coming out to a maze motion in the streets and going back when finished. Lesley cared for it, not for me.

'To those who can dream, there is no such place as far away'. Anonymous.

Yet another 'put your clocks back one hour'. Two days at sea. On Saturday, March 10 at 9.30 p.m. we were roused from our reverie by a sudden siren for a drill. This was for real. The ship had previously had several practice drills so we were instructed as to what to do. The first alarm was for the crew only. Nevertheless in the middle of watching a DVD in our pyjamas we donned warm clothing and shoes and we got personal documentation out of the safe, got our medications to the ready and waited. Thankfully five minutes later Capt. Jonathan announced from the bridge that the incinerator was giving up too much smoke and automatically sounded the alarm. 10 minutes later the all clear was sounded. A very professional approach, well done!

'Of all the books in the world, the best stories are found between the pages of a passport'. Unknown.

Ho Chi Minh City or otherwise known as Saigon, Vietnam was our next port of call. We docked at Phu My and a coach took us the 90 minute ride to the city. The road was lined with broken down stores, a few rice fields with water buffalo and egret birds. Vietnam is a long narrow country which borders on the east the South China Sea, to the north China and to the West Laos and Cambodia (Kampuchea) and further west is Thailand. It has suffered multiple invasions often with neighbouring countries. It was colonized by France in the mid-19th century and subsequently America. Its population amounts to 90 million and it has two seasons, hot and very hot. It has a huge American inheritance with the road signs in both English and Vietnamese and the traffic drives on the right. Hanoi, the capital city in the north, previously known as Thong Long was named after a dragon ascending. The rehabilitation of the country began in 1986 with fiscal reform. At present the economy is growing at 6% per annum and the median age is 28 years. It remains communist and education is paramount. In the south, Saigon has attracted international investment and now has the financial vibrancy of Hanoi. Our tour began in the militant Museum containing multiple statues of Buddha. Buddhism reflects multiple religions and ways of life. We were told about the multiple invasions and the Vietnam War which is now called the Civil War locally being the Vietcong versus the South. There were several tourist groups all very loud and drowning out our tour guides information despite a microphone. Our next visit was to a factory to see lacquered paintings, chinaware and chit chat. It was very touristy with elevated prices. The factory was all very congested and sweaty and again I resented being fleeced as a tourist. I think I was in a minority of one as it seemed very popular with my other companions. We then were taken to the sky deck which was a very tall building to be able to see over all of Saigon but the $10 charge was overpriced for the panorama by all accounts. I gave it the body swerve. All around were multiple high-rise skyscrapers downtown with new buildings everywhere. We lunched in a very fancy hotel and had a buffet with hundreds of similar visitors. I think some Americans need educated about what to stand in line or queue means. Politeness noticeably absent. We then saw the Opera house and the Notre Dame Cathedral from outside. The presidential palace was very impressive with a banqueting hall, cabinet room and a bunker below for protection if attacked. Once in 1975 a traitor flew over and bombed the palace creating some damage but not totally. We saw two residual tanks from the Civil War in the grounds. We then stopped at a cheap souvenir shop and were accosted physically by vendors selling cheap T-shirts and chit chat. We did not have US cash so did not buy anything. The tour guide advertised a book called the Tunnels of Cuchi authored in part by a BBC TV presenter describing how the Vietcong manoeuvred a subterranean approach to outwit the Americans in the war. I had to borrow $10 from a nice Canadian lady which I repaid when back on board. The next day was at sea which was a great rest!

'All that GLITTERS is not gold, all who wander are not LOST'. J. R. R. Tolkien.

Lesley was painting and I played bridge, with reading and writing and we saw that the hoses for the anti-piracy precautions had been removed. Every day at 10.30 am there was a walk around the periphery of deck 3 for a mile. Lesley did this every day and was joined by many others. For some the description was more a waddle than a walk. We are bound for Singapore.

We went through the Strait of Malacca which is the busiest sea lane in the world. After docking, to my consternation, I found the gangway was from deck three and involved several glass walkways but on this occasion I found the tingling and numbness with some dizziness of my acrophobia had ameliorated so perhaps things were improving. Again there were huge areas of reclaimed land on which multiple high-rises were being built. We took a boat on the Singapore River right in the centre of the city surrounded by impressive high-rise financials as well as old buildings from previous Indian and Chinese traders. The architecture was very impressive mixing avant garde with traditional. We visited a Buddhist temple and then went on to have a Singapore sling drink but unfortunately not at the iconic Raffles Hotel because this was being renovated. We drove through the Arab quarter and Chinatown. Overall Singapore is a very clean and tidy place with no litter or chewing gum and punitive charges for licenses for cars and scooters. This means the traffic is not nearly as heavy as other Oriental cities. They drive on the right and overall it is very westernized with a population of 5.6 million. Housing is very expensive. In the evening we went to the Marina Bay Sands Hotel which has 57 storeys. The sky deck according to Lesley provided amazing views over the city, I stayed in the lobby and had a beer. Then we took a trishaw around India town which was lovely and afterwards a repeat of the same river cruise but at night with lots of lights. The bars beside the river were packed with young people at night emitting a noise along with a band of about 150 dB's and again I wonder how they can communicate. There were also street performers entertaining the crowd. I certainly felt my age at that stage. Singapore started as a small fishing village and was spotted by Raffles who correctly identified it as a great trading post perfectly situated between East and West. It has a great harbour and freshwater supply from the Singapore River. Singa means lion and poura means city (Sanskrit) and hence the British named it Singapore. One of the early explorers thought he saw a lion but probably this was a tiger as there are no lions in the area. It is mainly a Buddhist religion followed by Malay and Hindu and many others. On our second day we went shopping via the underground and even the escalators move faster than elsewhere. The subway is very clean and efficient, the doors at the platform prevent people falling on the tracks which is a lesson that could be learned in London England. We took the wrong subway and ended somewhere at the terminus so returned and having drawn a blank at the shopping went to the Botanic Gardens. This was a haven of peace and quiet from the mayhem of the city. We had lunch near the orchid gardens. The food was very expensive and not very good. It would appear that foreigners have to pay to see the orchid gardens whereas locals are free.

'Bizarre travel plans are dancing lessons from God'. Kurt Vonnegut.

Phuket, Thailand is an island which is sweltering. We took a tour to the elephant Safari Park. We had a demonstration on how to grow rice and saw an ox with a plough to freshen the underwater soil. This was followed by sowing the seed, growing and whacking the grass to free the rice. This was then pounded. We then watched an elephant getting washed followed by a cooking class with Thai herbs. We were invited to smell some green sludge as a result but thankfully I could not smell anything. Then we had the treat of the voyage, a ride on an elephant. I had forgone the opportunity 25 years previously just outside Delhi. Another box ticked! Were also shown how latex was harvested from rubber trees and elephants that were trained to hunt bananas even when hidden in a tourists clothing. These elephants also threw darts at balloons with some accuracy. I felt somewhat uneasy at the spectacle almost as if in a circus. Lesley was not happy that the tour was not as advertised so we complained and had a partial refund. On return to the ship we met several stalls selling T-shirts etc.

'Travel is REBELLION in its purest form'. Anonymous

The next day was at sea to recover. The weather like all ports in that part of the world is febrile with incessant sweating (diaphoresis) the likes of which I could not remember as badly as this. I thought we had become acclimatized by this time. By this time we were in the Bay of Bengal.

'Every hundred feet the world changes'. Roberto Bolano.

Throughout our trip I was absolutely disgusted with the hectares of redundant adiposity fed by the wheaten Tsunami of the North Americans. The undulating quivering flesh offended my clinical eye and in particular the amount of carbohydrates ingested in the dining room. One could not help being disgusted by the gluttony of some passengers. Plates recurrently overloaded with food left half eaten with the eye larger than the stomach. Bowls overflowing with blueberries which led to shortages for other passengers. One couple both of whom were diabetic and hugely overweight seemed to survive on carbohydrates alone. Another American ordered two entrees at every meal in case she did not like one!

Colombo, Sri Lanka was hot and humid. However the mitigating factor was an easy gangway. We had a walking tour of old Columbia through a market, very busy and overcrowded and lots of Tuk Tuk taxis. These are essentially motor bikes with passenger seating. The island has been colonized by the French, Portuguese the Dutch and British. The tour began with a visit to the cabinet meeting and I felt angry that this consisted of several dummies sitting at a table. The tour guide thought this was highly amusing but I did not share his sense of humour. The stores in the streets were specialized in areas, for instance the bag street. Most of the stores sold bling for the tourists. We visited a mosque and were told that 7% of the population is Muslim. The religion is mainly Buddhist which is a philosophy rather than a religion. The languages spoken are Ceylonese, Tamil and English. The old fort has been converted to the Grand Oriental Hotel where we had a drink. The Civil War with the Tamil Tigers lasted 30 years and only finished in 2007. Sri Lanka means the resplendent island. They have reclaimed 275,000 ha of land by mainly Chinese workers. We saw the Pettah district. In the past were incredible bazaar streets teeming with oxen carts and alive with the sounds and smells of the sea. Multiple spices were on display contained by sacks arranged at the front of the street stores. The sensory overload was overwhelming. We saw the Jami Ul-afar mosque and the Khan Clocktower. Street stalls sell everything from textiles to electronics. The whole city was very vibrant. The commercial hub surrounded the fort. Vehicles were heavily taxed at 200% to avoid overcrowding. The heat was such that Lesley felt ill so we returned to the ship before the end of the tour. We missed the old Dutch hospital complex built in the 17th century which has now been restored to restaurant stores and bars. The old Dutch and English architecture has been maintained.

'The real voyage of discovery consists not in seeking new landscapes but in having new eyes'. Marcel Proust.

AROUND THE WORLD IN 113 DAYS.6

'Travel brings POWER and LOVE back to your life'.Rumi. TRAVELLING is not something you're good at. It's something you do. LIKE BREATHING'. Gayle Foreman.

Another three days at sea and we crossed the equator for the third time. Again there was the threat of Pirates so at night all lights were either turned off or curtains drawn. For instance on the sports deck no lights were allowed to play football. In 2009 there were several pirate attacks but none recently. We have constant plumbing problems with flushing and the cold water was extremely hot.. In about 200 to 300 AD Malays reached Madagascar in outriggers, hence the spread of civilisation. Our next stop was the Seychelles which is perfectly positioned for trading long before the Europeans. The unique fruit from here is the coco de mer. This is a fruit that takes two years to germinate and 6-7 years to mature. It weighs between 15 and 30 kg. It resembles an elephant's backside. The shell is the expensive part. Now the fruit has spread to India and the Maldives. The island was settled due to the Tradewinds in 1-3 AD and the discovery of sails. Vasco da Gama visited it. In 1608 a British East company ship was attacked off Zanzibar and escaped several storms heading southwest to land in the Seychelles in 1609. The first settlers discovered giant tortoises weighing 5 to 600 pounds. Pirates came from the West Indies to the Indian Ocean and raided enemy ships in their Corsairs. They were backed by France and as such if caught were regarded as the enemy and put into prisoner of war camps instead of being hanged as Pirates. Buccaneers were land-based hunters in the West Indies. Privateers originated from French British and Dutch and prayed on Spanish ships. When caught Pirates were hung high with a short rope to avoid waste of the rope. This meant they suffocated rather than suffering a broken neck which a longer rope produces. Today the dock was full of industrialized large ships and the view was marred by several wind turbines. The surrounding land rises steeply and forms an ideal harbour. Again the weather is unrelenting. We will remember the sauna when in the middle of snowdrifts this coming winter in Canada. The population is 72,000 and independence was gained in 1976. There are 115 islands 40 of which are granite and 75 coral. The exports are copper, cinnamon bark and vanilla. They are the oldest oceanic granite islands on earth. The centrally situated Clocktower in Victoria was a present from the UK but was dropped before installation and now the chimes do not work. I felt a bit ill so returned to the ship but Lesley continued the tour to the beach with lovely white sands, and the Botanics to see the coco de mer. Mahe is the capital of the Seychelles and the main industry is tourism on the south side of the island. Overall the tours were grossly overpriced. Unfortunately the exotic far Eastern ports did not match up to my high expectations and were somewhat disappointing.

'To live that is the rarest thing in the world. Most people exist, that is all' Oscar Wilde.

All the docks were ubiquitously populated by awesome huge cranes moving multitudinous lego like containers computerised to be precisely placed on board cargo ships. The scene is reminiscent of the outer space machines straight out of a scientific movie such as the War of the Worlds when the earth was invaded by Martians. Slow and careful are the watchwords and any aesthetic notions of the voyagers from the Amsterdam were totally dispelled by the confrontation of the docks initially changing the delights of the hinterland of the exotic countries. To join the Navy to see the world is to be condemned to frequent the sterility of rusting ugly pollution causing cargo ships.

'No matter WHERE YOU GO, there you are'. Buckaroo Banzai.

We were supposed to visit Madagascar to dock at Nosey Be but they were suffering from bubonic plague caused by the bacterium Pasturella Pestis, similar to the great plague of London with a very high mortality rate spawning the nursery rhyme 'ring a ring of roses'. At the time judges had a posy placed before them in court to cover the smell of rotting corpses as well as the classic ring rash heralding the onset of the disease. A fatal symptom involves sneezing and imminent death, hence the falling down. The Holland America line wished to choose the safer and financially wiser alternative of Reunion Island. We docked at St. Denis. The port is some way out of the city and the complementary shuttle bus took us along the coastal highway to St. Denis. From the docks the hillside graduates into a mountain shrouded by mist and clouds. Sightseers at the top could view the valleys briefly before being cut off by the moving colloidal mass. The sight we were told is beautiful to see. Housing was creeping up the gradient but stopping well short of the summit. The road was a switchback all the way up inducing motion sickness with some of the travellers. The new highway to the city has been built 50 yards offshore to avoid any falling rocks. Having reached the city we were underwhelmed by the paucity of points of interest, so the visit was very short-lived and pointless. After a few days at sea we were due to arrive in mainland Africa, the dark enigmatic continent.

'I read, I travel, I become'. Derek Walcott.

That night there was a celebration on board as the CEO of Holland America had embarked. Free booze and a band blasting from five to 6:30 PM. I personally was celebrating because it was 20 years to the day when I had my last cigarette. This was March 28, 1998 in Washington DC outside the Ritz-Carlton hotel!

'Work, TRAVEL, save, REPEAT'. An adventure.

All public areas in the ship are adorned with potted orchids immaculately maintained by two full-time florists.

'It is in all of us to defy expectations to go into the world and to be brave and to want, to need, to hunger for ADVENTURES to embrace change and chance and risk, so that we may be in know what it is to be FREE'. Mae Chevrollo.

Before the Civil War Lourenco Marques was loved by South Africans as a playground with wonderful seafood. The Civil War decimated Mozambique and changed the name of the capital to Maputo. When I was working in Natal there was an outpouring of Portuguese from their colony and it is claimed that the government was left bereft of intelligence and expertise which delayed the revival of the country. These days Maputo has not recovered and is frankly a dump. The government wanted $75 for a visa to step on their land so we stayed on the ship. The view was not very pleasant with ugly high-rise. Reports we got from those that visited were not good.

'We TRAVEL not to escape life, but for LIFE to escape us'. Anonymous.

Another day at sea and we were awoken at 5:30 AM to sheet lightning for half an hour. I was recalling my experience of my last visit to Cape Town 41 years previously. This was to sit the oral exam called the primary FRCS, the first stage in becoming a surgeon.

'You do not travel if you are afraid of the unknown. You travel for the unknown that reveals you within YOURSELF'. Ella Maillart.

We approached the dock in Cape Town and found a cargo ship in our berth so we had to wait for it to be moved. We were delayed for four hours and then had to form a long line for immigration. All passengers and crew had to go through whether they went ashore or not. In Cape Town at the time there was a drought and water was at a premium. I wanted to go to Stellenbosch to see the architecture and Vineland which I had not visited before. Thankfully the tour bus was rescheduled. The countryside is beautiful with vineyards all over the place. I visited Blaukippen winery (blue stone) which was very well kept. No need for the south facing slope necessary in Nova Scotia, there is enough heat and sun to ripen the grapes. I tasted six wines but all were very mediocre. There was a push to buy, but Holland America charged US$18 to take the wine on board, so it was not feasible. They did not ship to Canada. Then I visited Stellenbosch with a population of 150,000 people, Cape Town had 600,000 and the surrounding area 3.7 million. The Republic of South Africa has a total of 50 million population. The architecture of Stellenbosch has a good reputation but I was somewhat disappointed with the sporadic old buildings. There were several tourist curio shops, again very expensive. On the way home we passed corrugated townships with multiple satellite dishes. Apparently no animals were allowed although goats (sign of richness) abound. Kaleigha is the name of the township of forced displaced Cape Town dwellers which is quite a distance from Cape Town. In the meantime Lesley travelled to the top of Table Mountain via cable car hence I stayed at sea level. She said the *sights* were fantastic.

'Keep your EYES on the horizon and your nose to the WIND'. Clint Eastwood.

The next day we went on a safari (means journey) to Aquila Reserve (black eagle). We were supposed to start at 5:45 AM but there was no show from the driver. We began to think they had forgotten us but in fact the driver was told to pick us up at 6:10 AM which he did. A two hour drive would take us to the reserve. We almost didn't make it. We were driving along in the highway fast Lane at about 70 mph when a car in the slow lane appeared to drift off the road and then over corrected himself to cross 3 lanes and drive right in front of us, do a 180 degree turn and miss us by about 12 inches. If we had made contact I fear I would not be making this report. We passed through the Drakenstay and Du Toit mountain ranges and a 3mile tunnel. We eventually arrived for breakfast and in all the journey took us three hours. The safari was in an open truck with 13 people. He was a very good guide, black whose first language was Afrikaans but his English was very good. The first animals we saw were two male elephants. The African elephants have large ears which they flap to cool themselves, as well as hosing themselves with water from the trunk (they have two stomachs one for water and one for food) and sand and mud. The elephants have notoriously bad sight. While playing together the younger elephant appeared to grow a fifth rear leg. Once realization dawned on them there was hysterical howling laughter from the ladies at the back of the truck. The appendage continued to lengthen but with no recipient did not amount to anything. The elephants were surrounded by elands which are the largest antelopes in South Africa.. The next animals we saw were ostriches, the male is more beautiful than the female. The male has black feathers which warm during the day and give off heat to allow incubation of eggs during the night as the female does not incubate at night. Hippopotamuses were concentrated near a big Lake. These behave like ballerinas in the water and cannot swim. They require shallow water and kill more humans than any other mammal. They only attack if they are blocked from water when they become anxious as they have very sensitive skin and the water prevents rashes from the sun. They are vegetarians normally. The zebras are described as donkeys with pyjamas. They have digestive problems producing abdominal gas. They are beautiful animals and each marking is individual. We then saw lions in their own enclosure basking in a postprandial somnolence with apparent self-content. There were three southern giraffes which are noted for good eyesight and high blood pressure. Springboks were plentiful and identified with a black marking from their eyes like tear drops. There were also several rhinoceroses, the southern white type which are endangered. They have remarkably poor eyesight. The male deposits faeces with urine to form a solid ball which tells the female he is nearby. The ball is eaten by baby rhinos and zebras. We had an uneventful return and on the way back saw some black wildebeestes which are like camels, a mixture of many different animals. The big five is the name given to the most dangerous and difficult animals to hunt on foot which are African elephants, black rhinoceros, Cape Buffalo, African lion and the African leopard. The lion and the African bush elephant are classified as vulnerable. The leopard and the white rhinoceros are classified as near threatened. The black rhinoceros is classified as critically endangered.

'TRAVEL is about the GEORGEOUS feeling of teetering in the unknown'. Anonymous.

The reserve totalled 10,000 acres of which all was fenced in and the lions had their further enclosure. The headquarters contained a restaurant and several holiday rooms as well as rondavels which are thatched roofed small houses. They are often round. There was a group from Cleveland Ohio with families, the kids played rugby in a tournament locally and another group from the Wirral,

England with schoolchildren playing various games against locals. We thought this was excellent to open up the idea of understanding and tolerance of those who are not brought up in the same vein as these protected boys and girls. The Hottentots, one of the first races to inhabit the area, believe if you have a good life you will become a springbok in the next and a bad life makes you a wildebeest. Our guide also showed us that by rubbing quantitate stone against the iron rich Redrock and water produced a dark brown warpaint. On the way back to Cape Town we saw the floors of valleys covered with grapevines. Some had a Y trellis system blocking out the sun to the floor and reducing weeds. Some had nets but some had been harvested just recently. In parts vines stretched as far as the eye could see.

'TRAVEL. As much as you can. As far as you can. As long as you can. Life is not meant to be lived in one place'. The things we say.

The next day there was a thick fog on awakening. We visited a local mall, each mall seemed to become bigger in every port we visited but it was expensive. The adjoining market was full of cheap souvenir tat. On the way back to the ship the line up to have an exit stamp on the passport was tedious. There is another emergency drill on board and then we had a' sail away', a celebration of the visit. Back to a normal day at sea. It was a nostalgic visit for me after all this was a place where I first sharpened my scalpel, got incomparable experience and passed the first exam to become a surgeon. I will always have some feeling for the country.

'The eye never forgets what the heart has seen'. African proverb.

'Perhaps it was that the gangway from deck one was very easy to negotiate which kept me in a good mood.

'The IMPULSE to travel is one of the hopeful symptoms of LIFE'. Cherkasy.

Today it was Walvis Bay in Namibia. It garners a huge amount of rain at 2 inches per year. The day we visited was very foggy and overcast. About 7 km from Walvis Bay in Darob is the Dune 7 which is 92 -100 m high. Quite a sight. Then we went on to the

Mendoza Township. The tour was classed as "the real Namibia". We were shown the warts and all. The original Township had lots of shanties with corrugated roofs, walls of concrete blocks and some new buildings. Some had electricity and sewage but the new townships adjacent did not. For some there were communal toilets or outside toilets, others no electricity. There has been an influx from the hinterland of those seeking employment but unfortunately only too often this does not work out. The youth unemployment is 46%. Apparently each lot is 300 m² and the occupants can build themselves their houses but the government is stopping further potential tenants. We were entertained to traditional food including fried worms beans and spinach. I chose not to partake although Lesley did. We also enjoyed listening to a local choir of children singing traditional ballads. The population of this township was 65,000 but with abject poverty. Nearby is Swakopmunde which was a German colony prior to being taken over by South Africa. It was very helpful to the German war effort in the Second World War. It is now an expanding city with some lovely houses. Some fellow passengers went on 4 x 4 vehicles up and down the sand dunes giving them an exhilarating experience. The other industries are fishing and mining. The grinding unending poverty was reflected in the open air markets where all the state governed hygiene rules were ignored because it was a Saturday and no inspectors were working. Flies were ubiquitous covering dried fish and vegetables. Mounds of discarded clothing were laid out for sale to those unfortunates unable to afford better. The roads were unmade, dusty and worsened by the encompassing extensive sand dunes. The flat desert leading to the surrounding sand dunes reminded me of the movie 'Lawrence of Arabia' which was filmed where I worked in Northwest Saudi Arabia. Our tour guide emphasized that liberation from the colonial rule of South Africa gave the Namibians freedom. I could imagine he would be a leader in the revolution, however he was only eight years old on the day of independence in March 21, 1990. I did not want to go too deeply into the difficulties of setting up the independent state but he was confident in the future and on the face of it the country has vast resources with the potential of stability and economic viability although in my opinion this may take several generations. Overall we were impressed with Namibia and wish them well.

'TRAVEL far enough, you meet YOURSELF'. Cloud Atlas.

AROUND THE WORLD IN 113 DAYS. 7

'We live in a wonderful world that is full of beauty, charm and adventure. There is no end to the adventures we can have if only we seek them with our eyes open'. Jawaharlal Nehru.

Living in the enclosed cabin was not a problem for Lesley and I. She filled her sea days with painting, drawing, trivia team questions, bocce, putting and other should I say aimless activities. She loved the cruise if only to avoid thinking of meals, cooking, washing up and housework. For myself I had time to think, write and read. The self-discipline I had initially to read improving books gave way to reading page turners but overall it was satisfying my curiosity about those far-flung countries I had hitherto only read about. Essentially the cabin was only for sleeping and watching TV. We met only for meals during the day. The passenger list came to about 1200 but many did not do the whole cruise and only some segments. The crew numbered 400. I had great difficulty in coming to terms with the rudeness of some Americans who let down their nation. They obviously had no concept of being in an enclosed space for such a long time. They cannot be so selfish and inconsiderate of fellow passengers For instance we wanted to watch a movie and had some seats for friends. This was not acceptable to a loud mouthed American and his wife so they barged past us and sat in our friend's seats which they had temporarily vacated. He was wearing a Stetson hat obscuring the view of the passenger behind him. He was asked if he could remove the hat. "Perhaps" was the reply," if it is not too cold". And he had a huge head of hair. That is just one example. I think they would behave differently at home but maybe that is how they conduct their lives. I have complained but do not think the powers that be will do anything. Perhaps a strongly worded letter to the Seattle HQ of Holland America might be worthwhile. Perhaps it is me who is angry old man but at least I was brought up with manners as opposed to these louts.

'Like all great TRAVELLERS I have seen more than I remember, and remember more than I have seen'. Benjamin Disraeli.

Luanda, Angola is a city of opposites, or an oxymoron. They had an ongoing civil war beginning with independence in 1975 and was one of the most prominent armed conflicts of the Cold War. But now with peace they have found diamonds and oil offshore. It is billed as the most expensive city in the world (pardon the pun, a bill is a US dollar note). There are an enormous amount of new buildings with beautiful high-rise adjacent to rundown apartment blocks with external air conditioning throughout. Most investment has been Chinese funding which is extremely common in these emerging nations. The tour was designed to show the changing face of Luanda. Our first stop was the Igreje de Senhora de Nazare a small beautiful church that is a national monument. The streets were narrow and busy but not nearly as bad as some other cities we had visited. The old iron Palace was designed by the famous architect Gustav Eiffel. The Angolan national Museum of anthropology demonstrated an array of traditional masks, sculptures, tools, weaponry, jewellery, clothing and musical instruments. We visited the San Miguel Fort built in 1576 to defend the port from the French Spanish and Dutch invaders. The Agostino Netto Mausoleum, a huge stylized and rather impressive obelisk, is the gravesite of Angola's first president and was a gift from Russia. We saw the presidential Palace, the Prime Minister's office and the Ministries of Defence, Immigration, Justice, Health and the British Embassy. The parliamentary buildings were very impressive and similar to Washington's governmental edifices. The beautiful Catholic Igreja de Jesus church completed the tour. During the Civil War South African soldiers were fighting in Angola against Cuban Russian and Chinese soldiers as well as Angolans. The war finished when the rival Savimba leader of the rebel group died. Overall Angola is getting back on its feet from its previous Portuguese colonists and the Civil War but the Chinese seem to be taking a large part in the Renaissance. Luanda has a population of 1.5 million and Angola a population of 15 million.

'Live, travel adventure, place, and don't be sorry'. Jack Kerouac. Around the world in 113 days 8

'I travel because LIFE IS SHORT and the world is HUGE'. Stephanie B.

Another day at sea and at 6:30 am after my usual gym session I was sitting outside on deck three cooling-off and letting the sweat settle when I saw a school of dolphins about 20 of them off the starboard bow putting on a show for several minutes. It was quite spectacular. Having had a contretemps with an American over saved seats to watch a movie I suggested to the cruise director that he should have tickets made for popular events. He said that was a good idea and did nothing about it. We crossed the equator last night at 11:20 PM and at one stage our bow was in the Northern hemisphere and the Western Hemisphere and the stern was in the Southern hemisphere and the Eastern Hemisphere. So at last we had the Neptune ceremony which involved Neptune with the maiden Queen and the judge with a jury of ships officers. Various staff were found guilty and condemned to 'kiss the fish'. There were a couple of Americans who felt I should kiss the fish but when I saw what was involved, kissing a large frozen dead fish, I was pleased to have rejected their advances. The guilty people were covered in soapsuds and were condemned to sit under the broiling sun or to be thrown into the swimming pool. It was great fun and enjoyed by everyone.

'Travel is the frivolous part of serious lives, and the serious part of frivolous ones'. Anne Sophie Swetchine.

There was quite a change in the atmosphere of the ship since Cape Town with a lot of new faces, more grumbling and more confrontations amongst passengers. Most of the passengers were retired with obviously more interesting life experiences with a story to tell but the corollary is big egos and the American rights to everything at the cost to others.

Our next stop was Banjul in Gambia but we were delayed in docking because of a sandbar which slowed down the ship.

Our tour took us to the natural history Museum depicting the history of Gambia. Then on a short drive to the city to see the sights, stopping to visit the general market with much hassle and bustle. Anything from live chickens and vegetables, herbs and wigs can be bought and sold here. We stopped at the city's main mosque King Fahad mosque where children are inducted into Islam. Arch 22 was built to commemorate the coup d'etat of July 22, 1994 and independence. It spans Independence Drive at the entrance to the capital, Banjul. We then continued to Serre-Kunda, the most densely populated town in the Gambia. We saw tie- dyeing by locals and finally visited the Katchically crocodile pool where we met the famous reptilian resident, Charlie, who starred in a British television documentary. Lesley managed to stroke him without having to count her fingers afterwards. Religion is 98% Muslim and malaria is the biggest killer particularly in the wet season in summer. The vendors in the markets are extremely pushy. There is a huge disparity between rich and poor that even the middle class professionals, still have poor housing. It was assessed if you have a car you're very rich. There were mainly high-end cars of Mercedes BMW Porsche etc. the taxis were all Mercedes. The policy for the tour was to have police on the bus to ensure safety but we were assured this is the safest place in Africa.

'TRAVEL is still the most intense mode of learning'. Kevin Kelly.

In Senegal the capital was Dakar which is one of West Africa's largest cities. Our tour took us past the Catholic Cathedral, the Muslim mosque, the presidential Palace and various government buildings. The University of Dakar has 60,000 students, 40,000 are Senegalese and all faculties. We visited the Kermel market which again is a tourist trap and went on to the sand painting gallery. We saw an awe-inspiring monument to the African resistance movement. This was 160 feet tall of man wife and child which was to celebrate Senegal's 50 years of independence from France. We visited another mosque, the deity or divinity mosque. Again there was a huge disparity between rich and poor with several areas of corrugated hovels. It was a major part of the slavery trade. Again the vendors in the markets were very pushy and at times downright rude.

'Who lives sees, but who travel sees MORE'. Anonymous.

Overall by now we were getting tired looking forward to home and back to reality. There were 12 days to go. We had a talk from Andrew Schofield on David Livingstone which was excellent. He told us that slavery began in the 1400s until the 1800s. The first nation to initiate this deplorable behaviour was from Portugal. Livingston started trying to proselytise his belief on the unacceptable trade in slaves on the West Coast of Africa and eventually moved to the East Coast. Many of these slaves were shipped to America Brazil and the Caribbean. Although William Wilberforce managed to ban slavery in the UK in 1832 the trade did not stop until the late 1800s. The slaves were taken mainly from Gambia Senegal and Cape Verde. One tour visited Ile de Goree whose history comprises an integral part in the story of the slave trade. The history that wrested 40 million human beings from the shore of Africa was described. The slave house built in 1777 with its sales and shackles is still intact. Some visitors were left in tears by this tour.

'There are no FOREIGN lands. It is the TRAVELLER only who is foreign'. Cherkasy.

Cape Verde was the next stop on the Isle of Santiago with the capital of Praia. There wasn't really much to see in the town, a pedestrian street, a church in town square and again a vegetable market but as we were fully fed on the ship there was little point in the latter. The main centre is the Praca Alexandera Albuquerque square and we saw the statue of Diogo Gomes who discovered the islands in 1460. Again this was a centre of the slave trade. The worst offenders in the slave trade were in order Belgian, France, Portugal and then Britain.

'You will never be completely at home again, because part of your heart will always be elsewhere. That is the price you pay for the richness of loving and knowing people in more than one place'. Girlgi.com.

We were entertained by our fellow guests at an informal show with incredible talent amongst us. It was extremely funny and perhaps the highlight was a 22-year-old mongol girl who sang in her native Chek language as well as English. It is a little depressing to learn of the mortality rate amongst the passengers but I presume this is a reflection of the advanced age of the majority.

'BETTER TO SEE SOMETHING ONCE, than to hear about it a THOUSAND TIMES'. Asian proverb.

Our last port of call was Puerto Rico, almost home at last. The several large cruise ships disgorged over 10,000 passengers to flood the town. We were impressed with Puerto Rico which had almost completely recovered from the devastating hurricane a few months earlier but I believe the countryside was not so lucky. We saw the statue of Columbus in the centre of the town and a lot of the pristine buildings of government and offices. This could be a venue for snowbirds. A few more days and we're back in Fort Lauderdale, but with over 1000 people trying to get off the boat as soon as possible it was a bit congested but we were so pleased to be home with fond memories.

'I love the feeling of being ANONYMOUS'. Anonymous.

Overall we were very well looked after by the Captain, officers and crew as well as maintenance workers. They even went to the extent of issuing a note asking forgiveness for not producing an adequate toilet paper. The things some people moan about. On reflection we enjoyed our trip but with only staying a maximum of a few days anywhere we could not get into the culture very well. Perhaps we learned what places to revisit and what not to.

AROUND THE WORLD IN 113 DAYS 9

'Do it NOW. The FUTURE is promised to no one'.
Kushandwizdom.

The Flying Dutchman
Unyielding in the pride of his defiance,
Afloat with none to serve or to command
Lord of himself at last, and all by science,
He seeks the vanished land.

Alone, by the light of his one thought,
He steers to find the shore from which he came,
Fearless of in what coil he may be caught
On seas that have no name.

Into the night he sails, and after night
There is a dawning, thought there be no sun;
Wherefore, with nothing but himself in sight,
Unsighted he sails on.

At last there is a listing of the cloud
Between the flood before him and the sky;
And then—though he may curse the Power aloud
That has no power to die—

He steers himself away from what is haunted
By the old ghost of what has been before,--
Abandoning, as always, and undaunted,
One fog-walled island more.

Edwin Arlington Robinson.

'20 years from now you'll be more disappointed by the things you didn't do than by the ones you did do. So throw off the bowlines. Sail away from the safe harbour. Catch the trade winds in your sails.

EXPLORE. DREAM. DISCOVER

Mark Twain

'The most dangerous risk of all- the risk of spending your life not doing what you want on the bet you can buy yourself the freedom to do it later'. Unknown.

'I would rather own little and see the world and own the world and see little of it'. Alexander Sattler.

The following is a quote which hung on a wall at my home as long as I remember and which has guided me through good and bad times.

To know what you prefer instead of humbly saying 'Amen' to what the world tells you you ought to prefer is to have kept your soul alive.

R.L.Stevenson

As the Chinese curse says "may you have an interesting life."

Printed in the United States
By Bookmasters